Day Wa
North York **Moors**

20 circular routes in
North Yorkshire

VERTEBRATE **PUBLISHING**

Design and production by Vertebrate Publishing, Sheffield
www.**v-publishing**.co.uk

Day Walks in the North York Moors

20 circular routes in North Yorkshire

Written by
Tony Harker

Photography by **Adam Long**

Day Walks in the North York **Moors**

20 circular routes in
North Yorkshire

VG Copyright © 2011 Vertebrate Graphics Ltd and Tony Harker

VP Published by Vertebrate Publishing

ISBN 978-1-906148-32-4

Cover photo: Hawnby Hill.
Back cover photo: Robin Hood's Bay.

Photography by **Adam Long** unless otherwise credited.

All maps reproduced by permission of Ordnance Survey on behalf
of The Controller of Her Majesty's Stationery Office.
© Crown Copyright. 100025218

Design and production by Nathan Ryder.
www.**v-graphics**.co.uk

MIX
Paper from
responsible sources
FSC® C010256

Printed in China.

Contents

SKELTON TOWER - NEWTON DALE PHOTO: TONY HARKER

Introduction

The North York Moors National Park Authority describes the North York Moors as a 'very special place.' It may one of the smallest National Parks in the UK but it offers a network of paths and tracks packed unlike those in any other Park into high moorland plateaus and deep green valleys. Here the visitor will find England's largest expanse of continuous heather moorland, stretching from the Vale of York in the west to the stunning heritage coastline in the east.

The valleys cut predominantly north to south, with high and steep upland ridges running in between. To the north the Esk Valley bisects the park from Battersby in the west to the east coast at Whitby. Along this valley runs the Esk Valley railway; an umbilical cord bringing in tourists from Teesside, and serving those who live and work on the moors, stopping at places such as Castleton, Danby and Lealholm.

The Moors are at their most colourful during August and September, the tops smothered in a purple carpet as the heather blossoms in the late summer sun and the valley sides draped with rich green bracken and wild patches of bilberries. The Moors are steeped in mystic history too, a rich history which has left its mark with burial mounds, trods, stone crosses, abbeys and castles. More recently the workings of the industrial revolution are evident, particularly in Rosedale where the remains of ironstone mining are scattered around the valley.

My relationship with the Moors goes back to my teenage years where I learned navigational skills and developed my love for this fantastic wilderness 'playground.' Many paths were poorly marked – if at all – and I spent many hours 'heather bashing,' which in those days I didn't consider a hardship at all! In recent years the signage has improved dramatically and many paths have become well worn, making navigation for the less experienced just that little bit easier.

Many guides have been made available both in hard format and increasingly on the internet but there are still many places on the moors frequented only by inquisitive and determined explorers. Due to the availability of transport, more TV programmes promoting the 'great outdoors' and the increasing popularity of walking and mountain biking, the number of people visiting the moors is on the increase. Yet there are still places on the moors where the walker can find solitude and unspoilt paradise.

This guidebook will lead you to some of those places, where you can take a rest with only the sound of the wind carrying the haunting and evocative call of the curlew across the moor.

Tony Harker

Acknowledgements

Thanks to Doug and Karlyn Barlow, and Ian Lawson and Patrica Barcley-Lumb for accompanying me on some of these walks and testing others for accuracy. However, most of my gratitude goes to my wife Kay for her company on the majority of walks and despite all the detours we had to make due to her concern about passing through fields of cows!

About the walks

The walks described here are roughly between 5–14 miles and take about 2.5–6 hours to complete. Some are pleasantly short and provide a quick hit of moor ideal for a fine summer's afternoon.

All the walks are circular from a base where there is parking, public transport and facilities. Some can be based from a different start point if preferred and with a little planning a few can be linked to give a more challenging day out. For example, the two Goathland walks can be linked by omitting the Beck Hole and Mallyan Spout sections, and in fact this walk can even be extended to incorporate the Sleights route for a testing 20 mile day out. All the walks have a variety of terrain including high moorland and meadow. In a few areas it is probable that you will pass by herds of cattle in which case be sensible and don't linger. Some walks require careful navigation to stay on track so be sure you are comfortable using a map. On days of low cloud you may even need to use a compass or GPS. Most of all, these walks pass through a spectacular area of natural beauty and whichever walk you do you won't be disappointed.

The **summary** and route **description** for each walk should be studied carefully before setting out on a walk. Together they describe the terrain involved, the amount of ascent and the level of navigation skills required.

Walk times

The time given for each walk is on the generous side and based on a pace of around 4km per hour/2^1/$_2$ miles per hour, with time allowed for ascent and difficulty of terrain. There is some allowance for snack breaks and photo stops, but prolonged lunches should be added in.

Navigation

For most walks in this guide, following the route description in combination with the route map provided should be sufficient. However it is recommended you carry with you the appropriate *Ordnance Survey Explorer* series map as a back up. These are shown for each walk. The Moors are covered by two maps in the 1:25,000 series:

Ordnance Survey Explorer OL26 (1:25,000), North York Moors Western Area
Ordnance Survey Explorer OL27 (1:25,000), North York Moors Eastern Area

For moorland walks a reasonable level of map reading ability and competence in the use of a compass is strongly advised. If you possess a GPS (Global Postioning System) this can be a useful navigational aid in locating your position. However it is not a remedy for poor navigational skills.

Mobile phones

Although there is a degree of mobile phone reception over much of the area covered by the 20 walks, don't count on it. You may be left in peace by your phone, but you will also lack its support.

Footpaths and rights of way

All the walks in this guide follow public rights of way or other routes with public access, including *'permitted'* or *'concession'* footpaths.

Safety

It is strongly advised that appropriate footwear is used – walking boots designed to provide stability and security on uneven and slippery terrain. A waterproof, windproof jacket is essential and waterproof overtrousers or trousers are strongly recommended. Sufficient insulating clothing should also be worn or carried, that is appropriate to the type of walk planned and the time of year. Carry lots of food and drink, including an emergency supply. It's surprising how quickly you can become depleted and/or dehydrated, especially at the end of the day.

Mountain Rescue

In case of accident or similar need requiring mountain rescue assistance, **dial 999** and ask for **POLICE – MOUNTAIN RESCUE**. Be prepared to give a 6-figure grid reference of your position in the case of a moorland location.

The Countryside Code

Be safe – plan ahead

Even when going out locally, it's best to get the latest information about where and when you can go; for example, your rights to go onto some areas of open land may be restricted while work is carried out, for safety reasons or during breeding and shooting seasons. Follow advice and local signs, and be prepared for the unexpected.

» Refer to up-to-date maps or guidebooks.
» You're responsible for your own safety and for others in your care, so be prepared for changes in weather and other events.
» There are many organisations offering specific advice on equipment and safety, or contact visitor information centres and libraries for a list of outdoor recreation groups.
» Check weather forecasts before you leave, and don't be afraid to turn back.
» Part of the appeal of the countryside is that you can get away from it all. You may not see anyone for hours and there are many places without clear mobile phone signals, so let someone else know where you're going and when you expect to return.

Leave gates and property as you find them

Please respect the working life of the countryside, as our actions can affect people's livelihoods, our heritage, and the safety and welfare of animals and ourselves.

» A farmer will normally leave a gate closed to keep livestock in, but may sometimes leave it open so they can reach food and water. Leave gates as you find them or follow instructions on signs; if walking in a group, make sure the last person knows how to leave the gates.

» In fields where crops are growing, follow the paths wherever possible.

» Use gates and stiles wherever possible – climbing over walls, hedges and fences can damage them and increase the risk of farm animals escaping.

» Our heritage belongs to all of us – be careful not to disturb ruins and historic sites.

» Leave machinery and livestock alone – don't interfere with animals even if you think they're in distress. Try to alert the farmer instead.

Protect plants and animals, and take your litter home

We have a responsibility to protect our countryside now and for future generations, so make sure you don't harm animals, birds, plants or trees.

» Litter and leftover food doesn't just spoil the beauty of the countryside, it can be dangerous to wildlife and farm animals and can spread disease – so take your litter home with you. Dropping litter and dumping rubbish are criminal offences.

» Discover the beauty of the natural environment and take special care not to damage, destroy or remove features such as rocks, plants and trees. They provide homes and food for wildlife, and add to everybody's enjoyment of the countryside.

» Wild animals and farm animals can behave unpredictably if you get too close, especially if they're with their young – so give them plenty of space.

» Fires can be as devastating to wildlife and habitats as they are to people and property – so be careful not to drop a match or smouldering cigarette at any time of the year. Sometimes, controlled fires are used to manage vegetation, particularly on heaths and moors between October and early April, so please check that a fire is not supervised before calling 999.

CLIMB IT,
WALK IT,
PROTECT IT.

The British Mountaineering Council offers £10m of 3rd party liability insurance cover » we secure access to crags and uplands » we offer member discounts at over 600 outdoor retailers nationwide » we've been the only public voice for climbers, hill walkers and mountaineers in England and Wales since 1944 » we have 70,000 members, and the numbers are rising... join us.

THEBMC.CO.UK   0161 445 6111   members@thebmc.co.uk

Keep dogs under close control

The countryside is a great place to exercise dogs, but it is the owner's duty to make sure their dog is not a danger or nuisance to farm animals, wildlife or other people.

- » By law, you must control your dog so that it does not disturb or scare farm animals or wildlife. You must keep your dog on a short lead on most areas of open country and common land between 1 March and 31 July, and at all times near farm animals.
- » You do not have to put your dog on a lead on public paths as long as it is under close control. But as a general rule, keep your dog on a lead if you cannot rely on its obedience. By law, farmers are entitled to destroy a dog that injures or worries their animals.
- » If a farm animal chases you and your dog, it is safer to let your dog off the lead – don't risk getting hurt by trying to protect it.
- » Take particular care that your dog doesn't scare sheep and lambs or wander where it might disturb birds that nest on the ground and other wildlife – eggs and young will soon die without protection from their parents.
- » Everyone knows how unpleasant dog mess is and it can cause infections – so always clean up after your dog and get rid of the mess responsibly. Also make sure your dog is wormed regularly.

Consider other people

Showing consideration and respect for other people makes the countryside a pleasant environment for everyone – at home, at work and at leisure.

- » Busy traffic on small country roads can be unpleasant and dangerous to local people, visitors and wildlife – so slow down and, where possible, leave your vehicle at home, consider sharing lifts and use alternatives such as public transport or cycling. For public transport information, phone Traveline on 0871 200 2233.
- » Respect the needs of local people – for example, don't block gateways, driveways or other entry points with your vehicle.
- » By law, cyclists must give way to walkers and horse riders on bridleways.
- » Keep out of the way when farm animals are being gathered or moved and follow directions from the farmer.
- » Support the rural economy – for example, buy your supplies from local shops.

How to use this book

This book should provide you with all of the information that you need for an enjoyable, trouble free and successful walk. The following tips should also be of help:

1. We strongly recommend that you invest in the maps listed above on page ix. These are essential even if you are familiar with the area – you may need to cut short the walk or take an alternative route.

2. Choose your route. Consider the time you have available and the abilities/level of experience of all of members your party – then read the safety section of this guide.

3. We recommend that you study the route description carefully before setting off. Cross-reference this to your OS map so that you've got a good sense of general orientation in case you need an escape route. Make sure that you are familiar with the symbols used on the maps.

4. Get out there and get walking!

Maps, Descriptions, Distances

While every effort has been made to maintain accuracy within the maps and descriptions in this guide, we have had to process a vast amount of information and we are unable to guarantee that every single detail is correct.

Please exercise caution if a direction appears at odds with the route on the map. If in doubt, a comparison between the route, the description and a quick cross-reference to your OS map (along with a bit of common sense) should help ensure that you're on the right track. Note that distances have been measured off the map, and map distances rarely coincide 100% with distances on the ground. Please treat stated distances as a guideline only.

Ordnance Survey maps are the most commonly used, are easy to read and many people are happy using them. If you're not familiar with OS maps and are unsure of what the symbols mean, you can download a free OS 1:25,000 map legend from **www.v-outdoor.co.uk**

Here are a few of the symbols and abbreviations we use on the maps and in our directions:

 ROUTE STARTING POINT   **2** ROUTE MARKER    OPTIONAL ROUTE

52 ADDITIONAL GRID LINE NUMBERS TO AID NAVIGATION

PB = public bridleway; **PF** = public footpath; **GR** = grid reference.

Km/mile conversion chart

Metric to Imperial

1 kilometre [km]	1000 m	0.6214 mile
1 metre [m]	100 cm	1.0936 yd
1 centimetre [cm]	10 mm	0.3937 in
1 millimetre [mm]		0.03937 in

Imperial to Metric

1 mile	1760 yd	1.6093 km
1 yard [yd]	3 ft	0.9144 m
1 foot [ft]	12 in	0.3048 m
1 inch [in]		2.54 cm

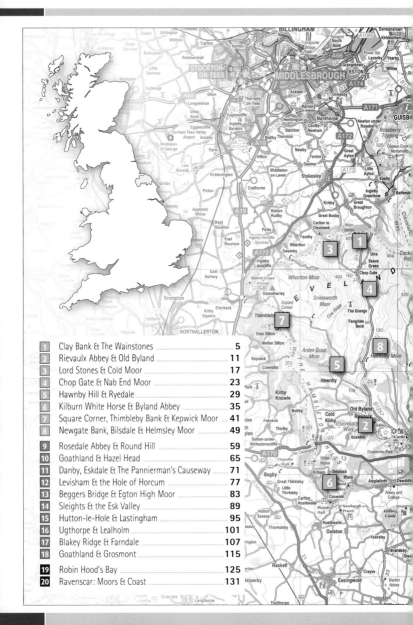

Day Walks in the North York Moors
Area Map & Route Finder

SECTION 1

Cleveland Hills & Hambleton Hills

The most western section of the moors is dominated by the pasture land plateau of the Hambleton Hills to the south and the line of steep sided Cleveland Hills at the northern edge. In between, the Ryedale Valley cuts north to south. Green fields and woods dominate the south while to the north the landscape is more rugged with extensive swathes of moorland.

VIEW FROM THE WAINSTONES

THE WAINSTONES

01 **Clay Bank** & **The Wainstones** 8km/5miles

Circle Hasty Bank past The Wainstones before climbing its opposite neighbour, Carr Ridge, via the seldom-visited slopes below the ridge.

Clay Bank » Hasty Bank » Wainstones » Urra » Urra Moor » Carr Ridge » Clay Bank

Start
Clay Bank car park. NZ 572035.

The Walk

The Wainstones, protruding from the western slopes of Hasty Bank, may not be as prominent as Roseberry Topping but on the Cleveland Hills they are a landmark that always attracts the eye when approached from the Tees Valley. The 'Steeple' and the 'Needle' stand prominent like two sentries guarding over the Cleveland Hills. The Wainstones provide a fascinating place to linger and explore on a warm day and watch the nimble athletes picking their way up the many climbing routes these crags have to offer.

We start the walk picking up the well-laid path alongside the forest, crossing the stile for the hardest climb of the day – 110m up the eastern slopes of Hasty Bank. We divert to take advantage of the southern protrusion offering a superb view down Bilsdale Edge and extensive views of the Tees Valley and across the Cleveland Hills and beyond to the Pennines. A steep drop between rocks leads down the ridge below the Wainstones and across the valley towards Cold Moor. Before the path turns steep we turn left through the bracken, crossing a shallow valley and joining the farm track past Whingraves.

After crossing the road we edge along a stream and climb to the small hamlet of Urra. From here the bridleway leads us bizarrely across a back garden – watch out for the washing – and then to a good track where we get a view of our second climb which (thankfully) looks harder than it is. The scenery here is a little more rugged as we reach the earthworks that provide the way to the end of Carr Ridge. Before we start the descent we ponder over classic views across to Hasty Bank. The descent is rocky and steep in parts, becoming easier on the lower slopes to the road and car park.

CLAY BANK & THE WAINSTONES

DISTANCE: 8KM/5MILES » **TOTAL ASCENT:** 380M/1,246FT » **START GR:** NZ 572035 » **TIME:** ALLOW 2.5 HOURS **MAP:** OS EXPLORER OL26 NORTH YORK MOORS WESTERN AREA » **REFRESHMENTS:** THE BUCK INN AT CHOP GATE; NEAREST CAFÉS IN STOKESLEY, OR LORD STONES CAFÉ AT CARLTON BANK » **NAVIGATION:** EASY AND WELL MARKED.

01 CLAY BANK & THE WAINSTONES

Directions – Clay Bank & The Wainstones

❻► **Turn left** briefly out of the car park onto the road for 230m. **Turn right** onto the stepped path signposted *Cleveland Way*.

2 After 160m **turn left** at the stile, climbing the eastern slope of Hasty Bank. 170m after the stile **turn left** onto a paved path. Follow this path for 90m **ignoring** the gully on the left and continue to the southern tip of the prominent edge. Follow the path around the edge and **turn right** at a small path junction leading to the main paved track on Hasty Bank.

3 At the Wainstones drop to the **right** on a path between rocks. Follow path into a dip keeping **straight ahead** at the gate. 30m from the gate **turn left** at the signpost to *Chop Gate*. Keep **straight ahead** at the next stile to a broken wall. From the wall **keep left** above reed beds and contour around to a wall at the far side of the stream leading to wall and stile. **Turn immediately right** over stile and continue **straight ahead** over the next stile leading to a farm track above Whingroves.

4 The track leads to a gate and forest. Follow the track past a waymarker, bending down to a stream and crossing **sharp left** to a gate and stile. Keep **straight ahead** over a field aiming for a stone pillar in the centre of the field and then to a double gate. From the gate keep **straight ahead** on a firm farm track to a track junction. At track junction continue **straight ahead** for 20m to a fence corner with waymarkers. Pass farm and cross to gate leading to shallow valley. Follow path through to road.

5 **Turn right** at the road for 10m and then **left** at the bridleway sign. Go down steps to bridge and keep **straight ahead** alongside fence. After 180m path leads into field and gate. Head for fence corner on left. From fence corner walk **straight ahead** across field to stile at top of hill. Keep between farm buildings to road, **turning left** on road for 20m.

►OR► **Optional Route (alternative finish):** Follow road around bend and then **turn right** at footpath sign. Follow waymarkers over fields above Mount House Farm. Cross stile to drop steeply into valley. 140m after stream crossing **turn right** at sign post. Climb hill alongside forest **turning left** at top. Follow track beside wall down to track. **Turn right** at track leading to road and car park.

6   **Turn right** at bridleway sign and then **quick left** at bridleway sign to gate in far corner of garden. **Turn left** onto double track. After 530m at wall corner the track bears to the right becoming a little indistinct: keep above the beck aiming for a gap in right-hand corner of field. **Cross the stream turning left** and then **sharp right** on wide grassy track.

7   Follow this track for 70m up between two hillocks and **bear left** at junction. This track climbs along a short ridge in line with trees: **bend/bear right** after the trees. Go **straight ahead** over track to gate.

8   After gate follow narrow path 160m climbing to bridleway on earthworks. **Turn left** for almost 800m to gate. Walk **straight ahead** at gate and drop down alongside wall to road. **Turn right** to return to car park.

RIEVAULX ABBEY

02 Rievaulx Abbey & Old Byland

10km/6.2miles

An easy-going walk from the former Cistercian abbey at Rievaulx.

Rievaulx Abbey » Rievaulx » Lambert Hag Wood » Low Gill » Old Byland » Tanker Dale » Nettle Dale » Rievaulx Abbey

Start

Rievaulx Abbey pay & display car park. Limited roadside parking. GR: SE 574849.

The Walk

The Hambleton Hills plateau extends eastwards splitting into many fingers of spurs and valleys reaching out into Ryedale. The magnificent ruins of Rievaulx Abbey sit at the bottom of two of these valleys and provide a stunning starting point to this easy walk. Here you can combine an easy woodland walk with some historical and cultural exploration.

Most of the views are north into Ryedale as we walk alongside the very old canal (constructed by monks to transport stone from the quarry to the Abbey site) and climb into Lambert Hag Wood. Once we are in Low Gill we have only trees for company, but it's pleasant and easy walking until the short steep climb to Old Byland. A short climb on a firm track takes us out to the road above Dick Wood from where we descend to the stream of Low Gill. From here we follow a soft wide track up the valley bottom to Old Byland. The road out of Old Byland brings us to our woodland descent down the lovely Tanker Dale to the stepping stones and ponds in Nettle Dale. A short bit of pleasant road walking brings us back to Rievaulx.

RIEVAULX ABBEY & OLD BYLAND

DISTANCE: 10KM/6.2MILES » **TOTAL ASCENT:** 240M/787FT » **START GR:** SE 574849 » **TIME:** ALLOW 3 HOURS **MAP:** OS EXPLORER OL26 NORTH YORK MOORS WESTERN AREA » **REFRESHMENTS:** TEA ROOMS AT RIEVAULX ABBEY; NEAREST PUBS IN HELMSLEY » **NAVIGATION:** EASY. LOW GILL IS BEST WALKED AFTER A PERIOD OF DRY WEATHER.

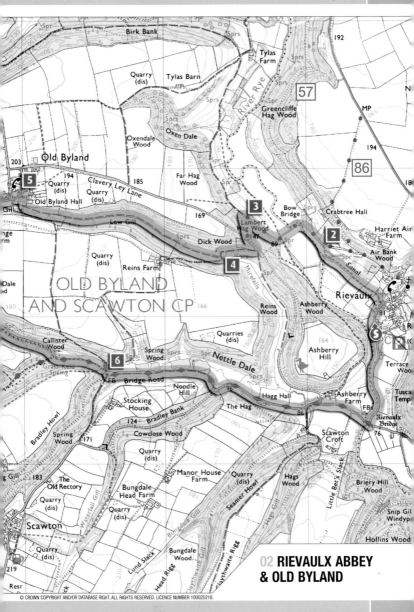

02 RIEVAULX ABBEY & OLD BYLAND

Directions – Rievaulx Abbey & Old Byland

➊ **Turn right** out of the car park towards the village. After 60m **turn left** onto the footpath signed *Bow Bridge*. A sequence of three gates leads into the field alongside the canal.

➋ After 600m the path joins the narrow lane via a single gate. **Turn left** to Bow Bridge. Cross the bridge and after 160m **turn right** on a firm track.

➌ **Turn left** after 300m and follow the lane to the road. **Turn left** for 100m and then right onto a bridleway. At the bottom of the hill **cross the stream** and then **turn immediately right** onto double track.

➍ Stay with this track for 2km **ignoring** any tracks leading off to the left. At GR 549857 look for a short steep track to the right. Turn off **right** here and climb up to the road at Old Byland. (If you miss this turn continue on and follow the track climbing to the road 100m further along.)

➎ **Turn left** onto the road. After 1.4km look for bridleway sign at road bend. Cross stile and **turn left** onto firm forest track. 500m down the valley **keep left** at track junction. Stay with this track for 1.35km to opening of valley and sharp track bend. **Turn off left** and then **immediate right** at blue waymarker, through gate and over stepping stones.

➏ **Turn left** on track and follow for another 400m to road. **Turn left** for 1.1km over bridge. **Turn left** for 700m to return to car park.

COLD MOOR

03 **Lord Stones** & **Cold Moor**

11km/6.8miles

Explore the secluded Raisdale before climbing the heights of Cold Moor and Cringle Moor with their panoramic views north over the Tees Valley.

Lord Stones » Raisdale Mill » Cold Moor Lane » Cold Moor » Cringle Moor » Lord Stones

Start

Lord Stones Café. If you're not using the facilities you can park on the road side. GR: NZ 523029.

The Walk

Raisdale is one of the less well-known valleys on the moors. While only stretching for 5km from Carlton Bank to Chop Gate it offers good views and beautiful scenery and you may not see another walker until reaching the summit of Cold Moor. The final section from Cold Moor and over Cringle Moor is part of the Cleveland Way, the Lyke Wake Walk, the White Rose Walk and the Coast to Coast! A well-trodden path indeed! The views from here northwards extend over industrial Teesside and beyond, and on a clear day the Pennines can be seen lurking to the west.

Leaving the edible temptations of Lord Stones behind we take the easy going footpath over meadows above the line of Raisdale Beck. This leads us to a short walk through Raisdale Mill Plantations and then on to Raisdale Mill itself. We cross the field towards Crossletts Farms before our first climb of the day to the road junction below Stone Intake. Further footpaths cross fields and stiles to lead to Cold Moor Lane. This climbs gradually to Cold Moor ridge where we enjoy terrific views all around as we trek 1km along the spine to Cold Moor summit on the edge of the Cleveland Hills.

We don't need to linger to admire the view as it stays with us while we drop down from Cold Moor, with an old jet mine just over our shoulder to the left. We are left with one last climb onto Cringle Moor, made easy with carefully laid steps, and soon we are striding out towards the viewpoint. We finish the walk with a 1.5km downhill to the Lord Stones Café and eagerly awaited refreshments.

LORD STONES & COLD MOOR

DISTANCE: 11KM/6.8MILES » **TOTAL ASCENT:** 400M/1,312FT » **START GR:** NZ 523029 » **TIME:** ALLOW 2 HOURS
MAP: OS EXPLORER OL26 NORTH YORK MOORS WESTERN AREA » **REFRESHMENTS:** LORD STONES CAFÉ; THE BLACKWELL OX INN, CARLTON » **NAVIGATION:** EASY AND WELL MARKED.

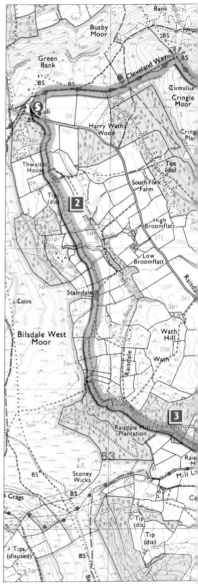

03 LORD STONES & COLD MOOR

Directions – Lord Stones & Cold Moor

➏ From the Café **turn left** onto the road and then after 30m **turn right** onto a farm road signposted *Thwaites House*. Follow this road to Thwaites House at 350m and then go **straight ahead** through a gate into a field marked as a public footpath.

2 After the dip and crossing a wide track, **keep to the right** up the bank before dropping down to a wooden footbridge. From the bridge stay with the footpath keeping left with the fence leading to another farm road. **Turn right** and pass through the farmyard into a field and follow the path for 500m to a single gate. Go **straight ahead** at a single gate and keep **straight ahead** passing a stone barn to the right. After the barn pass through two gates and keep to the edge of the woods. Just after the end of the wall **bear left** and angle down the field to a double gate leading into the forest. **Turn left** on the forest road.

3 After almost 500m metres **turn right** onto a wide grassy track which soon narrows. Follow this path through to Raisdale Mill. **Turn right** after the first building. Follow the road around a right bend after the buildings and then up the hill for 80m before **turning left** over a stile. Cross this field via a wide grassy track for 200m to a gate at the far side. After the gate keep **straight ahead** through a short patch of bracken and then across the field keeping to the wall to the farm lane. (Don't drop into the woods.) **Turn left** and walk up the hill to the road.

4 Go **straight ahead** over the road for 150m and **turn right** onto a farm track towards the farm. As you enter the wide gravelled farmyard **turn immediately right** to a double gate. Go through this gate and **turn left** passing the farm building on the left. After almost 500m **turn right** at an opening in the bracken and walk downhill to a gate and the road.

5 At the road bend **turn immediately left** over the stile. Walk across the field, with the wall to the left, and over another stile. At the next corner **turn left** through the gate and **immediately right** through the adjoining gate and follow the path down the field to another gate. After this gate **turn left** bearing up the hill for 200m to a stile at the top. **Turn right** after the stile and follow the path to a bridleway track (Cold Moor Lane).

6 **Turn left** up the track. Stay on this bridleway through a double set of gates after 150m and then on to the moor gate after another 200m. Follow the path past the woods and steadily climb to the ridge on Cold Moor (1.5km from moor gate). **Turn right** onto the wide track and follow it north for 1km to Cold Moor summit.

7 At the summit **turn left** down a paved path – the Cleveland Way – towards Cringle Moor. At the bottom of the hill **keep right** with the wall corner to a gate. Pass through the gate and **turn left** and then **left again** at a fork after 250m. Follow the Cleveland Way climbing Cringle Moor and west over the moor to the viewpoint. After the viewpoint stay with the Cleveland Way down the hillside back to Lord Stones.

RAISDALE MILL

FORD AT SEAVE GREEN

04 **Chop Gate** & **Nab End Moor** 12km/7.5miles

A varied walk along Nab Ridge with stunning views into Bilsdale, before a pleasant return along the edge of Bilsdale West Moor.

Chop Gate » Seave Green » Nab End Moor » Hill End Wood » The Grange » Bilsdale West Moor » Chop Gate

Start

Chop Gate car park (including toilets). GR: SE 559993.

The Walk

It can be difficult to decide which way round to do this walk. I have opted for clockwise as this offers the easiest route up Nab Ridge followed by stunning views into Bilsdale on the walk south down the ridge. The terrain is varied, and the brief walk through Hill End Woods is wonderful, as is the easy amble on the west side of the valley with its terrific views into the north of Bilsdale.

We leave the unusually named Chop Gate north through the village passing the Buck Inn. From Seave Green we follow a rough footpath through a small *secret valley*, eventually leading to and climbing steadily onto the open hillside. We can see our route up ahead while the views open out towards Hasty Bank and Cold Moor behind us. Once on Nab End Moor we turn south down the ridge with easy walking on a well defined track. The rocky outcrops along the deep valley side of Tripsdale can be seen to the east, but the view south remains hidden until we reach the oversized cairn at the southern point of the ridge.

Here, the Bilsdale valley opens up in front of us and, if we look carefully to our right just after the cairn, we should see the remains of a stone circle said to mark the location of a Bronze Age burial chamber. The walk down the ridge becomes steep as we dip into woods and the dramatic drop through Hill End Wood.

We complete the walk by crossing the B1257 and picking up a network of marked bridleways and footpaths on the lower slopes of the western side of the valley. Not as dramatic as Nab Ridge but with constant views towards the Cleveland Hills.

CHOP GATE & NAB END MOOR

DISTANCE: 12KM/7.5MILES » **TOTAL ASCENT:** 380M/1,246FT » **START GR:** SE 559993 » **TIME:** ALLOW 3.5 HOURS **MAP:** OS EXPLORER OL26 NORTH YORK MOORS WESTERN AREA » **REFRESHMENTS:** THE BUCK INN, CHOP GATE; LORD STONES CAFÉ, CARLTON BANK; PUBS AND CAFÉS IN STOKESLEY » **NAVIGATION:** MOSTLY EASY AND WELL MARKED.

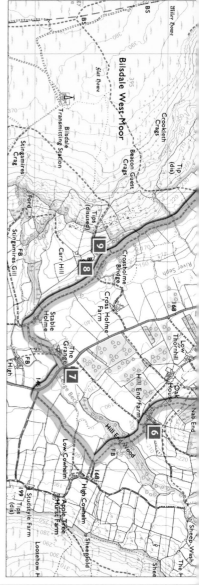

04 CHOP GATE & NAB END MOOR

Directions – Chop Gate & Nab End Moor

➎► Leave the car park on the road heading north through Chop Gate passing the Buck Inn. Stay with the road for another 760m turning **right** at Seave Green.

2 Turn **immediately right** at a bridleway post crossing a ford. After 260m **turn right** off the track (opposite stile with yellow marker) cutting across a rough field to the **right** for 60m to a footbridge. Cross a bridge and **turn left** through gate.

3 Follow this path through the valley for 200m and **turn left** over a beck and then **immediately right**. Trace the wall/fence up a gentle bank for 200m to a field corner. **Turn right** under a sign, cross a stream and then **turn left** to a multi signpost. **Keep left** from the signpost on a wide grassy track between gorse.

4 After 300m go through a gate and **turn immediately left** up alongside a wall. Follow the wall through another gate and after 150m **bear right** following a track in a shallow gully leading to a gate with a public footpath marker. After the gate double track leads to the ridge. **Turn right** on a track along the ridge south for 1.1km to a large cairn.

5 Keep heading south from the cairn as track becomes narrow leading to sheep pen and then alongside wall bearing right. As the path drops **turn sharp left** into forest for 100m. **Bear left** at footpath marker at the edge of the forest into a gully. (Don't be tempted by more defined path bearing to the right.) Path leads to Hill End farm with a public footpath waymarker showing the route to the **left** through farmyard.

6 Shortly after the farm **turn left** through a gate into a field. Follow the path near to the wall on the left to a large stile leading to woods. Stay with the narrow path descending steeply, keeping **right** at a tributary and then **left** to footbridge. After the bridge pass through a gate and **keep ahead** to far side of fields and a gate to a lane. **Turn right** at lane for 650m to B1257. **Turn right** at main road.

7 After 250m **turn left** on lane at post box signed *Public Bridleway*. (**Note**: it is safer to walk down the road and cross after the bridge at the lay-by.) Follow the lane for 460m and then **turn right** passing Stable Holme and then **slightly left** onto a path in a shallow gully past a gate. Now follow the marked public footpath for almost 500m to a farm road.

8 Turn left after a gate on a grass track next to a farm road. Cross the cattle grid and follow the track around the back of buildings to a stile.

9 From the stile go **straight ahead** and follow the path marked by public footpath waymarkers for 900m, climbing to a wall and gate. Walk **straight ahead** at the gate and follow an indistinct path **bearing left** over a field picking up a rutted track to High Crookleith Farm. After the farmyard **turn right** down to a bridge and, when approaching Low Crookleith Farm, **turn right** on lane. (Right of Way is diverted and different to map.)

10 After 130m **turn left** at public bridleway sign into field. Cross the field and **turn right** at a stile. Follow bridleway for 440m to Orterley Farms. Keep **straight ahead** with buildings on your right to a gate and double track. Keep **straight ahead** on footpath for 590m to a stream crossing. **Turn right** on a good path to return to the car park.

THE GRANGE

HAWNBY HILL CRAG

05 Hawnby Hill & Ryedale

13.5km/8.4miles

A great walk through Upper Ryedale, crossing Hawnby Hill and Hawnby Moor.

Hawnby » Low Wood » Blueberry Wood » Brewster Hill » Hawnby Moor » Ladhill Beck » Hawnby Hill » Hawnby

Start

Hawnby Village. Roadside parking is very limited in the village but there is more space on the lower road at Dalicar Bridge. GR: SE 542898.

The Walk

Hawnby village sits tight below Hawnby Hill, one of the two distinctive hills in the upper end of Ryedale. The hills sit side by side and are almost identical in size. While Easter Hill is the higher of the two at 310m it is Hawnby Hill that is the final target of this walk and it provides an excellent high ridge finish to this splendid walk through upper Ryedale.

We leave the small village of Hawnby on a farm track heading north parallel with the River Rye. After crossing the Rye we head towards Blueberry Hill before crossing a deep valley and meeting our first testing climb of the day; Brewster Hill. From the farm we find ourselves back into the trees at Green's Wood before dropping back down to the Rye, which we cross via a substantial footbridge. A short easy walk from the bridge brings us to the Osmotherley/Hawnby road: we may linger to view the waterfall at the road bend before we cross a field dropping into the woods and crossing a shallow ravine via a footbridge. The ravine can be quite dramatic after heavy rainfall!

From the bridge we meander through the woods to the moor edge before following a path from the ruins up the side of the woods. Further up the hillside we head out over the moor to views opening up across to Easterside Hill. Good tracks lead us into the valley below Crow Nest where we cross Ladhill Beck. A steep climb from the bridge brings us to the road where we may have to call on remaining energy reserves for the steep climb onto Hawnby Hill. This final effort is more than worthwhile as we are rewarded with a wonderful 360 degree panorama along the ridge before dropping to finish in Hawnby.

HAWNBY HILL & RYEDALE

DISTANCE: 13.5KM/8.4MILES » **TOTAL ASCENT:** 500M/1,640FT » **START GR:** SE 542898 » **TIME:** ALLOW 4 HOURS
MAP: OS EXPLORER OL26 NORTH YORK MOORS WESTERN AREA » **REFRESHMENTS:** HAWNBY STORES AND TEA ROOM; THE INN AT HAWNBY » **NAVIGATION:** MOSTLY EASY AND WELL MARKED, HOWEVER CARE IS NEEDED ON CLIMB OVER HAWNBY MOOR.

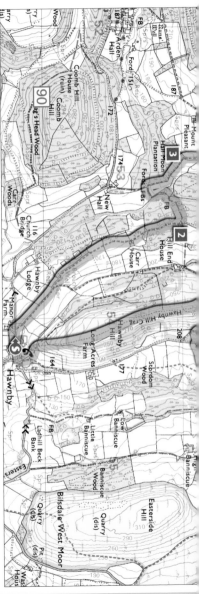

05 **HAWNBY HILL & RYEDALE**

Directions – Hawnby Hill & Ryedale

➊ Leave the village heading west past The Inn at Hawnby for 200m, **turning right** signed *Public Footpath* onto a farm track. Follow the guide arrows for 1km to Carr House. Keep left and drop across a field past a post with a marker into Low Wood.

2 200m into the woods **turn left** at bridleway and follow this downhill to a bridge. Cross bridge and follow path and markers to track. **Turn right** through Half Moon Plantation.

3 At end of woods join farm track. 160m after gate and stream crossing **turn left** at *Public Footpath* signpost. Climb hill angling across the field and cross the fence via a gate. Continue up next field and **turn right** onto firm track.

4 After 360m at wide track junction keep **straight ahead** dropping down the hill to a fence. Follow the path downhill to a footbridge and up a steep climb to Brewster Hill. Keep farm to right and follow path **bearing left** onto narrow path into Green's Wood.

5 320m through woods cross gate into field and follow path down towards river. Drop to riverside and **turn right** at bridge climbing to farm buildings. Follow track **turning left** after buildings to gated track to road. **Turn left** at road for 160m.

6 **Turn right** at stile and footpath sign. Cross field over another stile into woods. Follow path down to bridge. Cross bridge and **bear left** on track climbing slightly for 160m to woods edge. After stile **turn immediately right** past barn climbing up along forest edge.

7 After 370m path leads onto Hawnby Moor **becoming a little indistinct. Aim for track just to left of shooting butt 100m ahead.** (In poor visibility use compass bearing or GPS.) Stay on this defined track for 680m to track junction on Round Hill.

8 At the track **turn right** and then **immediately left** at guidepost. The path is indistinct for the next 420m. Again use bearing or GPS aiming for wall corner. From the wall follow well defined sandstone track down to ford. 800m after ford bear right and southerly.

9 After 600m as track bends to left **turn off right** onto a peaty defined track still heading in a southerly direction. After another 600m **turn right** at track junction. Stay with this track to gate at 360m.

10 Pass through gate and keep **straight ahead** on this track for 900m leading to a ford. Cross ford and **bear right** and then **left** on a well defined track leading up the hillside to the road. Cross the road and walk **straight ahead** for 20m **turning right** on a track. After 200m **turn left** onto a path leading up the hillside. After 50m **turn right** again onto a steeper path leading to the top of the ridge. Follow the path south on the ridge, picking up the public footpath on the lower slopes above Hawnby. **Turn right** and **right** again, into the village.

KILBURN WHITE HORSE

06 **Kilburn White Horse & Byland Abbey**

16km/10miles

A great summer day walk from the iconic White Horse, taking in ancient ruins, expansive views and five pubs.

Kilburn White Horse » Kilburn » High Kilburn » Byland Abbey » Mount Snever » Cockerdale Wood » Shaw's Gate » Hambleton » Kilburn White Horse

Start

White Horse car park. GR: SE 514812.

The Walk

The White Horse, gliders, wide views, ancient ruins, the site of an old battle and five pubs – what more could you want?! This is a great summer day walk offering an easy route over meadows and woodland while still reaching a height of 300 metres. The walk along the escarpment to the glider club offers a fine finish with extensive views to the west and north over the crags beyond Sutton Bank. If you're one for regular refreshment then there are five pubs to choose from along the way.

We leave the car park, head down the hill and along the road into Kilburn village. From Kilburn we follow well-marked footpaths across meadows, meandering around the low hills of High Kilburn to the magnificent ruins of Byland Abbey. After the Abbey the first climb of the day leads up to the ridge of Abbey Bank Noddle and Mount Snever. On the ridge we enjoy lovely woodland walking, meandering through the woods with views south over the Vale of York.

After the wide pasture to Cam Farm a wonderful path winds down through Cockerdale Wood and eventually to Cockerdale Farm. On the long steady climb through woods to Shaw's Gate we pass the little chapel at Scotch Corner, the site of a Scottish victory over the English in 1322. A little road walking leads to the path to the escarpment edge just to the south of Sutton Bank. The path is well maintained and easy to follow past the glider club and above the White Horse. A steep stepped path drops down past the horse back to the car park.

KILBURN WHITE HORSE & BYLAND ABBEY

DISTANCE: 16KM/10MILES » **TOTAL ASCENT:** 500M/1,640FT » **START GR:** SE 514812 » **TIME:** ALLOW 5 HOURS **MAP:** OS EXPLORER OL26 NORTH YORK MOORS WESTERN AREA » **REFRESHMENTS:** CAFÉ AT MOUSEMAN VISITOR CENTRE, KILBURN; FORESTERS ARMS, KILBURN; ABBEY ARMS, BYLAND ABBEY; BLACK SWAN, OLDSTEAD; THE HAMBLETON INN, SUTTON BANK ON THE A170; WOMBWELL ARMS, WASS » **NAVIGATION:** PATHS EASY TO FOLLOW AND WAYMARKED.

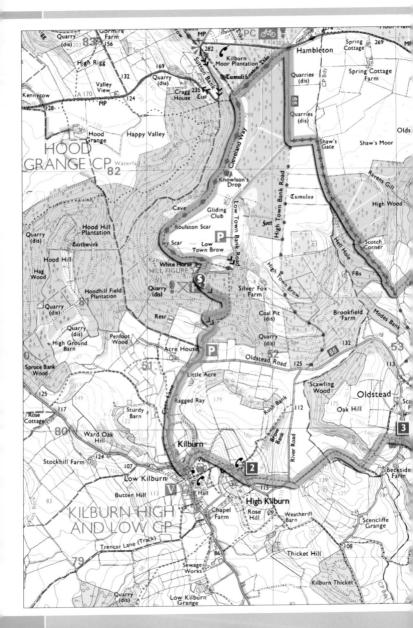

06 KILBURN WHITE HORSE & BYLAND ABBEY

Directions – Kilburn White Horse & Byland Abbey

➤ Leave the car park heading down the road into the village of Kilburn. In Kilburn **turn left** at the Foresters Arms and follow a path through the churchyard to the lane at the top of the hill. **Keep left** at the lane and go past the green at High Kilburn.

2 **Turn left** onto a footpath for 300m, cutting the bend of the road. Go **straight ahead** over the road onto a wide track. Follow this for 650m through to a three-way sign-post and **turn left** dropping to a footbridge. Keep **straight ahead** after the bridge uphill to a waymarker post. At the top of the hill cross a stile and **keep left** along the edge of the field. At a point 70m after the stile, and 50m before a telegraph pole, **turn right** onto a footpath angling across the field towards a stile and gate to the road.

3 Keep **straight ahead** passing the Black Swan pub to the right. After 240m, at the road bend, **turn right** onto a farm track signed *Public Footpath*. Follow this track through to Oldstead Grange. Follow footpath signs past the Grange **keeping left** after the stream following footpath signs to Cam Head.

4 Now follow signs for *Byland Abbey* for 1.2km to the road. **Turn left** on the road passing the Abbey Arms and the ruins. **Keep right** on the road for 170m and **turn left** towards Abbey House. **Almost immediately turn right** over a stile. Cross a field to another stile and then follow a path to the uppermost corner of the field to a gate behind a bench. Keep **straight ahead** to lane.

5 At the lane **turn left** for 320m (the lane becomes a forest track) to a track junction. Go **straight ahead** onto a footpath signed *Cam Farm*. After 360m at top of the field **turn left** onto a track into forest signed *Cam Farm*. This track meets another track after 390m. Keep **straight ahead** here up a steep embankment signed *Public Footpath* and follow a slippery path for 70m to the ridge.

6 **Turn right** on the ridge on a narrow path re-joining a forest track after 300m. **Turn right** and keep **straight ahead** for 300m to the forest edge. Cross a stile into a wide field and follow the footpath to Cam Farm. Go through a gate to the **left** of the farm and follow waymarkers past Cam House to a gate.

7 Keep to the **left** path after gate dropping to forest edge. Walk **straight ahead** at gate into forest and after 140m keep **straight ahead** at junction. 10m after junction **turn left** at *Public Footpath* sign onto narrow path through trees. Follow this path for 300m, dropping to track. **Turn right** on track for 50m then **left** through gate to field. Follow this path across field to Cockerdale Farm.

8 Pass the farm following waymarkers on a wide track which becomes indistinct – keep **left** up the field to a double gate. **Turn right** on track and follow this for 1.5km past Scotch Corner to the road. **Turn right** at the road for 700m to a point just before the A170 and **turn left** on path signed *Cleveland Way*. After 500m **turn left** at escarpment edge and follow a good path – still the Cleveland Way – to the White Horse. **Turn right** after the Horse down steps to the car park.

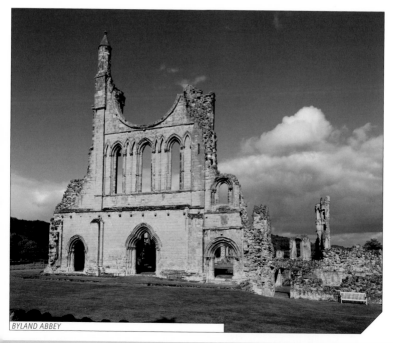

BYLAND ABBEY

SQUARE CORNER, THIMBLEBY BANK & KEPWICK MOOR

DISTANCE: 19.8KM/12.3MILES » **TOTAL ASCENT:** 580M/1,902FT » **START GR:** SE 479959 » **TIME:** ALLOW 5 HOURS **MAP:** OS EXPLORER OL26 NORTH YORK MOORS WESTERN AREA » **REFRESHMENTS:** THE COFFEE POT, OSMOTHERLEY; VARIOUS PUBS IN OSMOTHERLEY; THE GOLD CUP, NETHER SILTON » **NAVIGATION:** PLENTY OF WAYMARKERS BUT TAKE CARE AFTER THE OUTCROP ON THIMBLEBY BANK THROUGH TO OVER SILTON.

07 Square Corner, Thimbleby Bank & Kepwick Moor

19.8km/12.3miles

A variety of woodland, pasture and moors walking on the north westerly tip of the North York Moors.

Square Corner » Big Wood » Thimbleby Bank » Over Silton » Nether Silton » Nab Farm » Kepwick Quarry » Locker Bank » Dale Head » Square Corner

Start

The rough car park at Square Corner. GR: SE 479959.

The Walk

This route covers a variety of terrain with forest, woodland, meadows and expansive moorland. The views change throughout the walk and the church near Over Silton and the old Kepwick limestone quarry add historic interest. The wide Drovers Road high on Black Hambleton has history, being one of the main routes used by farmers to get their animals to market. Alas only ruins remain of the Limekiln House Inn.

Starts don't get much easier than the downhill walk into Oakdale. The path is wide, reinforced and easy to follow with terrific views over the reservoir below. After climbing sharply up the steep slope to Big Wood, we get a quick glimpse of Osmotherley village and the Pennines before meandering through the woods to the outcrop on Thimbleby Bank and a magnificent view. From the outcrop we continue through the woods to amazing views of Black Hambleton and Kepwick Moor.

Pasture walking around Over Silton leads to the 12th Century Norman church, both quaint and magical. More pasture walking leads to Over Silton and the old tramway before our second climb of the day. Here we get views across to Kepwick Quarry and the old tramway. The climb leads to the wide expanse of the Drovers Road where we head north to White Gill Head (possible shortcut back to Square Corner). Continuing north around the contours of Locker Bank the tops of Carlton Bank and Cold Moor appear on the northeastern horizon, but it is not until we turn down Locker Moor that the full view can be had: north over expansive moors to the Cleveland Hills, the valley of Arns Gill and deep into Ryedale. Surely one of the best vistas on the Moors. The views remain as we descend Low Locker Moor to Dale Head. An oversized bridge, presumably built to take horses, leads safely over Bawderis Beck before a climb, track and road back to Square Corner.

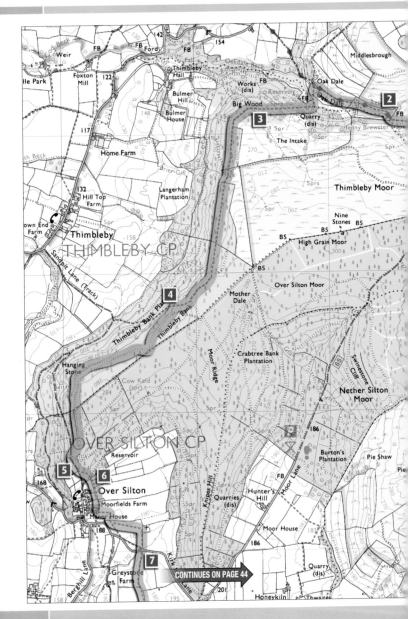

CONTINUES ON PAGE 44

07 **SQUARE CORNER,
THIMBLEBY BANK &
KEPWICK MOOR (PT 1)**

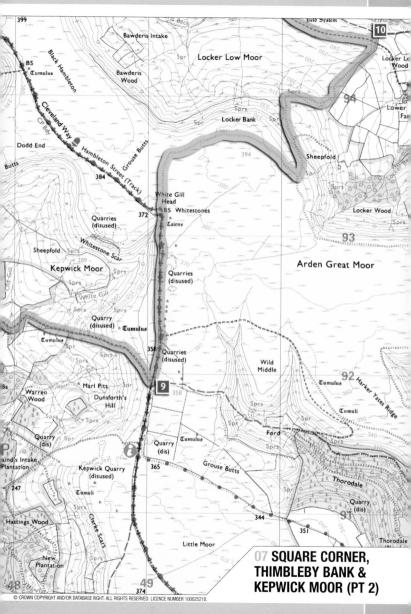

399

BS
Tumulus
Black Hambleton
BS

Bawderis Intake

Bawderis
Wood

Locker Low Moor

Field System

10

94

Locker L
Wood

Locker
Wood

Cleveland Way

Locker Bank

Lower
Fa

Dodd End

Hambleton Street (Track)

Grouse Butts

Sheepfold

Butts

384

394

Sheepfold

Locker Wood

White Gill
Head
BS Whitestones

93

372

Cairns

Quarries
(disused)

Whitestone Scar

Sheepfold

Sprs

289

Arden Great Moor

Kepwick Moor

White Gill

Quarries
(disused)

Quarry
(disused)

Tumulus

Tumulus

358

Quarries
(disused)

Wild
Middle

92

Harker Yates Ridge

Tumulus

Tumuli

Warren
Wood

Marl Pits

Dunsforth's
Hill

9

358

Ford

Quarry
(dis)

Tumulus

P

Quarry
(dis)

i

and's Intake
Plantation

Kepwick Quarry
(disused)

365

Quarry
(dis)

Grouse Butts

Thorodale

247

Tumuli

Quarry
(dis)

91

Hastings Wood

Clarke Scar

344

351

Thorodale

New
Plantation

Little Moor

48

49

374

**07 SQUARE CORNER,
THIMBLEBY BANK &
KEPWICK MOOR (PT 2)**

Directions – Square Corner, Thimbleby Bank & Kepwick Moor

➲ Leave the car park heading west and walk straight over the road at the *Cleveland Way* signpost. Follow this well laid path for 560m down to the footbridge, keeping **straight ahead** at the path junction halfway down.

2 From the bridge follow the track alongside the reservoir for 600m. Just before the buildings **turn left** at a short post and follow a line of trees onto a path to a gate and footbridge. After the bridge the path starts a steep climb and opens out at the top after 400m. (**Note:** This path is diverted and different to the route on the OS map.)

3 **Turn right** at the top of the climb for 60m to a gate, then **turn left** onto a path for 100m to a viewpoint. **Turn left** and follow all *Public Footpath* signs for 1.5km through the woods to a large rocky outcrop. (**Note:** The last 300m of this path is different to the OS map). From the outcrop keep **straight ahead**, starting to drop down the hill.

4 After 90m at a lone silver birch tree **turn left** onto a less well-defined path. The track, rough in places, turns and rises briefly to meet a track junction after 400m. **Turn right** here, again dropping downhill. Follow this for 1km to meet the forest road.

5 After 90m, where the track bends sharply to the right, follow it around and cross over to the wall edge and bridleway. **Turn left** and then **left again** after 90m onto indistinct footpath. Follow the path through woods bending left in and out of the gully to a forest track at the woods edge. (Don't worry if you lose the path, just keep heading southeast.)

6 At a wide track cross **straight ahead** over a stile into a field. Stay on this path over a series of stiles for 260m to a point where the path turns sharp left at a waymarker. The right of way crosses the back of private gardens to a stile. **Turn right** onto a concrete lane. The lane leads to a gate after 60m. After the gate **turn left** onto a path for 250m over a field to a church. **Turn right** at the wall to the road.

7 Go **straight ahead** over the road onto a footpath. Follow waymarkers for 660m to Nether Silton and cross the road to a white gate. Shortly after the gate, at the edge of a building, cross into the next field and pick up a wide track downhill to the bottom field corner. **Turn left** over a ditch and fence and then **immediately right**. Now follow the footpath and waymarkers for 650m to a wooden bridge crossing Bridge Beck. Follow path alongside fence for 300m to a wider track: **turn left** and follow track through tunnel of trees to road.

8 **Turn left** at road for 500m and then **right** onto farm lane. The lane leads to Nab Farm. Pass the farm to the right via two gates onto farm track. The track bends to right dropping to beck after 470m. Cross beck and **immediately turn left** onto a track leading uphill to a gate. Keep **straight ahead** at gate and follow track around the woods and then alongside wall to the top of the climb.

9 Pass through double gate and **turn left** onto wide Drovers Road. After 1.2km cross cattle grid and, when track bends to the left, keep **straight ahead** on double track. **Turn left** after 1.5km onto rough double track. Follow this track **turning right** after 550m and leading to wall and down to bridleway crossing by gate.

10 At gate on right **turn left** onto bridleway over moor to substantial footbridge over Bawderis Beck. Climb hill (waymarked) towards building, passing the building to the left and onto track. Follow track to road and **turn left** back to car park.

FAIR HILL FARM AND EASTERSIDE HILL

08 Newgate Bank, Bilsdale & Helmsley Moor

22km/13.7miles

A demanding walk, requiring good navigation skills, that rewards with stunning scenery in some of the most remote corners of the Moors.

Newgate Bank » Easterside Hill » Low Ewe Cote » Hagg End » New House » Laskill Moor » Helmsley Moor » Bogmire Hill » St Mary Magdalene Church » Cowhouse Bank Wood » Rievaulx Bank » Newgate Bank

Start

Newgate Bank car park (including toilets). GR: SE 564889.

The Walk

An easy start from Newgate Bank gives terrific views over the valley towards Easterside Hill, which we then climb gently on a sequence of footpaths past Fair Hill Farm and across the River Seph. A panorama opens up from the summit, but we bear east and begin our first navigation over open moor and the descent to Low Ewe Cote. Pleasant meadow walking leads over the Seph again, before a stiffer climb into woodland and above the old quarry workings (fantastic views over Bilsdale) and on to the ruins at New House.

Our second section of open moor from New House begins on a shooting track in a shallow valley before dirt track over Laskill Moor.

We follow the track around the edge of Helmsley Moor joining the footpath over Bogmire Gill. The farm on the hillside here is one of the most remote working farms on the moors.

Easy track and road walking leads to the final moor crossing, also the most demanding due to the lack of a distinct footpath. On a southeasterly bearing heavy heather walking leads to the beautiful spot at the stream crossing over Bonfield Gill, before easy waymarked walking brings us to the quaint and isolated St Mary Magdalene Church. Navigation eases from the church, with wide tracks through Cowhouse Bank Wood and on the climb up Rievaulx Bank to the plateau on Rievaulx Moor. A final 2km bash along the tree line edge gives extensive views south into the Vale of York, and more dramatic views over the moors to the north.

NEWGATE BANK, BILSDALE & HELMSLEY MOOR

DISTANCE: 22KM/13.7MILES » **TOTAL ASCENT:** 620M/2,034FT » **START GR:** SE 564889 » **TIME:** ALLOW 6 HOURS **MAP:** OS EXPLORER OL26 NORTH YORK MOORS WESTERN AREA » **REFRESHMENTS:** PLENTY OF CAFÉS AND PUBS IN HELMSLEY » **NAVIGATION:** GOOD SKILLS NEEDED IN PLACES.

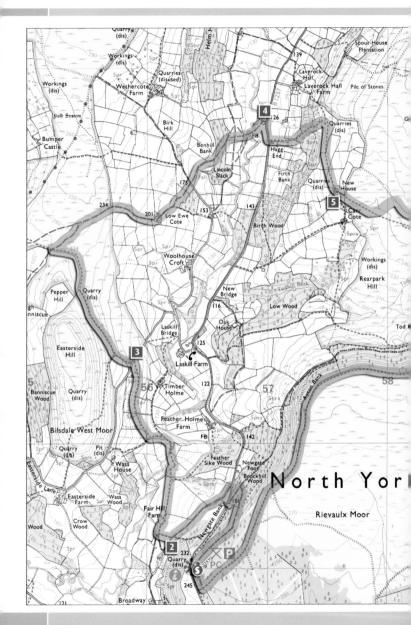

08 NEWGATE BANK, BILSDALE & HELMSLEY MOOR

Directions – Newgate Bank, Bilsdale & Helmsley Moor

➋ Head down the bridleway from the roadside edge of the car park **turning left** at the forest track at the bottom. **Turn right** at the road for 150m and then **left** onto a marked bridleway.

2 After 650m **turn right** at a stile and head down a field towards a fence and farm. At the fence **turn right** (**do not** cross the stile) and follow the path alongside the fence for 150m. **Turn left** at the gate and then **right** to the next gate. Go **straight ahead** at this gate into a field, keeping to the right of the tree line. After the second tree **bear slightly left** down to a footbridge. Cross bridge, climb hill to barns and then follow track **left** with wall. After 100m **fork right** with path tracking the wall for 660m to road.

3 **Turn left** for 50m and then **right** up steps to a footpath. Follow the footpath for 1.2km to a gate on the left. **Turn sharp right** onto bridleway leading to a wall and gate after 600m. Walk **straight ahead** at gate and follow *Public Bridleway* signs past Low Ewe Cote and then to the lane end. Keep **straight ahead** on track past forest edge. Just 10m after gate **turn right** (**not signposted**) to footbridge and then follow path to road.

4 **Turn right** for 140m and then **left** at *Public Footpath* sign before building. Follow signs across short fields leading to woods. After 140m **turn right** with a path climbing above the woods. **Turn right** at top path and follow waymarkers to the ruins at New House.

5 At the ruins **turn left** between the buildings on a track leading to moor gate. Keep **straight ahead** on footpath. (**Note**: difficult to follow. If you want to stay in line with the footpath over the moor take a bearing or head for the forest corner of Roppa Wood.) **Turn left** after about 270m and the shooting butt, and meet double track. **Turn right** on track and follow it to the corner of Roppa Wood and a track junction. Keep **straight ahead** on a track towards Collis Ridge, bending left after 1km and dropping to a wall above Bogmire Gill. (**Note**: The footpath over Helmsley Moor is an option but most of it is indistinct.)

6 At the wall **turn left** for 60m and then **turn right** over a stile. Follow the footpath down the valley to a footbridge and climb the hillside to Piethorn. Pass the farm onto farm track which leads to a road after 1.5km (**ignore** all turnings). **Turn right** on road for 450m. **Turn left** onto the moor at the *Public Footpath* sign and *'Potable Water Shed'*. Navigate the line of the footpath over the moor – **mostly indistinct** – to Bonfeld Gill. (**Note**: there is a path but this gradually leads too far to the east. Keep southeast and some heavy heather walking will take you to the beautiful stream crossing over Bonfield Gill.)

7 Cross the Gill and **turn right** over a stile, with a waymarker, to a footpath. After 180m **turn right** on path leading after 300m to a gate. **Turn right** on dirt track before next gate and follow this to a ford. **Turn left immediately** before the ford at a waymarker. Stay with this footpath alongside a wall leading to Lund Farm. Pass the farm to a track junction and go **straight ahead** at forest and **keep right** at single gate past St Mary Magdalene Church to road.

8 **Turn left** and then **right** at lane to ford. **Keep left** after ford for 400m to Old Ford. Keep left around house and **straight ahead** at iron gate. Follow this path ascending for 1.5km to a track junction. Keep **straight ahead** on firm forest track for 360m to a junction and fence corner. **Turn left** uphill on a clay track leading to firm track on the plateau. **Turn right** and follow this track for 2.8km back to the car park.

EASTERSIDE HILL

SECTION 2

Central Moors

The central moors are dominated by the three main valleys of Bransdale, Farndale & Rosedale with Bransdale being the quieter of the three. To the north of these dales the Esk valley cuts east to west dotted with lovely moorland villages such as Commondale, Castleton and Lealholm, all linked by the Esk Valley railway. The high tops between the valleys are smothered with heather, purple splendour in the summer with blankets of rich green fern draping the valley sides. In the autumn the colours change to a kaleidoscope of browns and oranges lasting into the winter months. This area is a wonderful place to explore but the walker always needs to keep an eye on the weather as these moorland tops can all look the same in poor visibility with few landmarks to aid navigation.

THE VILLAGE OF ROSEDALE ABBEY, AND ROSEDALE

THE TRACK DOWN SWINE STYE HILL

09 Rosedale Abbey & Round Hill

10.5km/6.5miles

A circular walk from picturesque Rosedale Abbey exploring the remote North Dale and a disused railway line.

Rosedale Abbey » North Dale » Swine Stye Hill » Round Hill » Thorgill » Rosedale Abbey

Start

The car park east of Milburn Arms in Rosedale. Also parking either side of Milburn Arms and around the village green. GR: SE 725959.

The Walk

Rosedale Abbey is just about in the centre of the North York Moors, making it one of the most suitable places to base a walk from. The village itself is quaint and tidy with a pub, tea rooms, post office store and caravan site. However it is the valley in which it sits that attracts the visitors. Steeped in mining history, yet beautiful, the valley offers a number of options for walkers. The walk described here is easy, using both sides of the valley on a variety of paths and the old railway.

We leave Rosedale Abbey from behind the Milburn Arms heading into the lovely but little frequented North Dale. The path tracks Northdale Beck across a succession of fields and stiles but is well signposted. A short climb takes us out of North Dale and we drop back into Rosedale via a pleasant wooded track and cross the valley via Craven Garth Farm.

The climb ahead on Round Hill over the valley is visible but looks harder than it is. At the top we can relax on the old railway with magnificent views into the valley. A narrow path takes from the railway into the head of Thorgill. It's a little boggy crossing the gill but a good path guides us down to the hamlet. From here we cut over a field joining Daleside Road briefly, before taking a path crossing a short field to the campsite and back into the village.

ROSEDALE ABBEY & ROUND HILL

DISTANCE: 10.5KM/6.5MILES » **TOTAL ASCENT:** 350M/1,148FT » **START GR:** SE 725959 » **TIME:** ALLOW 4 HOURS **MAP:** OS EXPLORER OL26 NORTH YORK MOORS WESTERN AREA » **REFRESHMENTS:** THE COACH HOUSE, THE ABBEY TEA ROOM AND MOLLY'S FARM SHOP – ALL ROSEDALE ABBEY; WHITE HORSE FARM INN, CHIMNEY BANK; SMALL VILLAGE STORE » **NAVIGATION:** MOSTLY MARKED. CARE IS NEEDED AFTER CROSSING THE BECK IN THE FOREST.

09 ROSEDALE ABBEY & ROUND HILL

Directions – Rosedale Abbey & Round Hill

❺ From the car park follow the footpath through the double gate heading up the valley into North Dale. Keeping the stream to the left a well signposted footpath leads through a succession of gates and stiled walls to the lane in North Dale.

2 Cross the lane slightly **left** onto a narrow path angling up the field. Pass the pond and barn on your right before joining the track at the edge of the woods. **Turn left** to the road.

3 **Turn right** at the road for 30m and then **left** onto a forest track. Follow this for 600m where the track turns into single track. After 200m bear **sharp left**, crossing stream. After crossing two deep gullies **do not** stay left with the main obvious track but **bear slightly right** and follow the track through woods to a stile at the woods edge. **Turn right** and follow the track past Clough House. After 300m **turn left** and drop to the road.

4 **Turn right** at the road for 200m and **then left** at the Orange B&B. Follow this lane down through Craven Garth farmyard and then **straight ahead** into a field. This path leads into the far corner where you need to cross a stile leading to a footbridge. After the footbridge the path turns **left** and climbs to a track.

5 Go **straight ahead** over the track and keep to the **left** of a boggy piece of ground heading for a metal gate at the top of the field. As you near the gate **bear right** onto a path bending slightly left up the hillside leading to the old railway.

6 **Turn left** onto the disused railway. After 1km, just after the fenced shaft to the right, **turn off left** at the footpath sign choosing a narrow path. Cross the stream after 550m **keeping left** at the white post on the opposite bank. Stay with this path keeping **straight ahead** for 500m to a double gate. **Turn left** to single gate onto a gravelled road bending right.

7 **Turn right** at a fence corner before tarmac road to a single gate with waymarker. Follow this path with wall to your left, dropping to road after 570m. **Turn right** on road for 600m.

8 **Turn left** onto a footpath across to the far right-hand corner of field. Go through single gate to steps bearing **right**, over bridge to campsite. Follow campsite road briefly **turning left** at a yellow waymarker between fences. Follow into village keeping **straight ahead** to car park.

ROSEDALE

GOATHLAND STATION

10 Goathland & Hazel Head

An easy walk over moorland and pastures with waterfalls, steam trains and wonderful scenery.

Goathland » Mallyan Spout Hotel » West Beck » Hazel Head » Julian Park » Carr Wood » Beck Hole » Darnholm » Goathland

Start

Goathland car park. GR: NZ 833013.

The Walk

This short loop starting in Goathland packs a lot of varied walking into its 11km and, although there is almost 400m of ascent, the climbs are short. The alternative route to Thomason Foss is highly recommended, but it can be dangerous in parts and may not be ideal for the unsure footed. Enjoy fantastic scenery all around on this magnificent walk.

We start from the car park taking the road east towards the Mallyan Spout Hotel. From here we pick up a classic winding moors path contouring above Hunt House Road on the lower slopes of the moor. The path offers good views over towards Wheeldale Moor and the valley of Bumble Wood. After the moor the terrain turns to pasture as we cross West Beck before the biggest climb of the day to Hazel Head Farm.

A short bit of road work leads us to a wonderful path through Carr Wood. The path meanders through the trees dropping into the charming hamlet of Beck Hole and an opportunity for refreshment at the famous Birch Hall Inn. If you are in a group larger than six there won't be much room for you in the bar! From Beck Hole the more adventurous can enjoy the rough track towards Thomason Foss Falls. The more sheepish will climb to the safer moors path. Both routes lead us on to the beautiful ford area at Darnholm before we finish above Goathland Station (watch for the steam train!) taking the road back to our start.

GOATHLAND & HAZEL HEAD

DISTANCE: 11KM/6.8MILES » **TOTAL ASCENT:** 360M/1,181FT » **START GR:** NZ 833013 » **TIME:** ALLOW 3 HOURS **MAP:** OS EXPLORER OL27 NORTH YORK MOORS EASTERN AREA » **REFRESHMENTS:** THE GOATHLAND ARMS, THE MALLYAN SPOUT HOTEL, THE INN ON THE MOORS, GOATHLAND TEA ROOMS, THE MOORS TEAM ROOMS – ALL GOATHLAND; BIRCH HALL INN – BECKHOLE » **NAVIGATION:** MOSTLY WELL SIGNED, BUT FREQUENT REFERENCE TO MAP IS RECOMMENDED ESPECIALLY OVER THE MOORLAND SECTION.

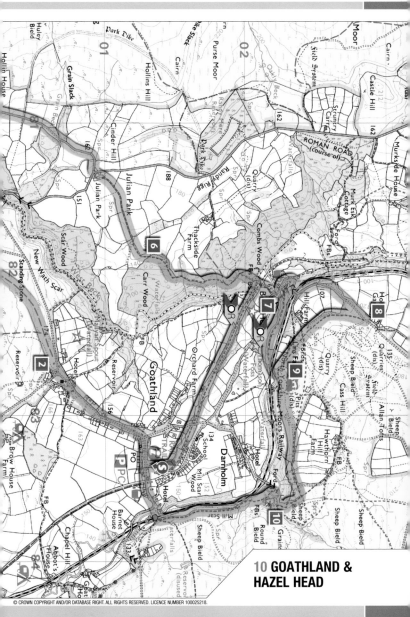

10 GOATHLAND & HAZEL HEAD

Directions – Goathland & Hazel Head

⑤ From the main car park **turn right** to the main road and then **right again**. Follow the road for 1km to the road junction at the Mallyan Spout Hotel. **Turn right** at the junction and then after just 10m **turn left** onto a grassy track signed *Public Bridleway*.

② Follow this track contouring above Hunt House Road. The track becomes narrow and is a delightful walk around the moor with views opening up over Wheeldale Moor. After 1km the path forks: take the narrower **left fork** climbing the hillside towards a tall cairn.

③ At the cairn there is a small quarried area: **turn right** past the cairn onto a rock path following the edge of the escarpment and marked by cairns. **Bear right** after the last cairn in line, about 800m after the first one. The area is marked with a wide expanse of rocks. Follow the path down the hill strewn with rocks aiming for the left corner of the wood ahead.

④ **Turn right** briefly on the road for 180m and then **turn left** onto a wide track sign-posted *Roman Road* leading downhill through two gates to the concreted ford over West Beck. **Turn right immediately after the ford** before the metal gate following the bridleway arrow. This path leads up the hill to Hazel Head Farm.

⑤ Pass through the farm area through a double gate onto the lane. Follow this lane for 1.6km past Hollin House farm to a sharp right bend and road at Julian Park. **Turn left** and then after buildings **turn right** onto footpath. Stay with this footpath through the field **ignoring** left fork after 180m. The path turns left with the wall after another 480m and drops down to a stile leading into Carr Wood.

⑥ This is a delightful path through the woods. Follow for 800m **turning right** at the signpost for Beck Hole. The path drops sharply down stone steps crossing West Beck again, through a gate onto the road at Beck Hole.

> **OR** At this point just after the bridge you have the option of the easier route back by **turning right** onto the Railway Walk track which takes you directly back to Goathland.

7 **Turn left** past the Birch Hall Inn and cross the bridge.

> **OR** This is the more dramatic alternative. After the bridge **turn right** at the footpath and follow this up alongside a sharp edge eventually dropping alongside the stream. After 350m **turn left** up an earthy climb through the trees to a fence and railway. (Keep **straight ahead** with stream to view waterfalls and return). **Turn right** at fence and follow under bridge climbing to bench and wall corner. **Turn right** at path (rejoining main walk at point 9).

8 570m after the last sharp left bend, just before the farm, **turn right** onto the footpath. Follow for 400m to a wall corner and **turn right**. Drop downhill for 90m and **turn left** at the footpath sign. This path leads to another wall corner with a bench after 400m.

9 **Avoid** going straight ahead dropping to the valley but instead take the grassy path to the **left** gently climbing the contours to Lins Farm. Pass the farm and after the double gate **turn sharp right** down through the bracken and steps, over the bridge and onto a wide gravel track.

10 **Turn right** at the track towards the ford. Don't cross the ford but **turn left** just before the ford over the field. The path leads to steps climbing the side of the steep valley side. Follow this path over the top above the railway, eventually dropping down to the station gate to the **right**. Cross the railway and continue straight up onto the main Goathland road **turning right** back to the car park.

11 Danby, Eskdale & The Pannierman's Causeway

11.5km/7.1miles

This route is short enough for a casual summer afternoon walk and would be ideal for the family with a variety of terrain.

Danby Moors Centre » Clither Beck » Pannierman's Causeway » Danby Park » Castleton » Ainthorpe » Danby Moors Centre

Start

Danby Moors Centre car park (pay and display). GR: NZ 717083.

The Walk

Danby is well placed centrally in the northern sector of the National Park. It is surrounded by high moors to the north and open dales to the south, with the central moors beyond. The valley of Clither Beck is delightful and the walk over Rosedale Intake with its views and heritage is as good as any moorland path in the National Park.

After leaving the car park we go straight onto a footpath alongside the lovely babbling Clither Beck. This takes us up some easy climbing to Clitherbeck Farm. From here we cross the road onto the moor leading over to Rosedale Intake. After crossing the ford over Ewe Crag Beck a short climb rewards with fine views into Danby Dale as we drop into the Esk Valley. A good path leads through the lovely Danby Park before a short road walk up the hill to Castleton village. After refreshments we follow a network of footpaths over fields with great views across the Danby Moors and west up the Esk Valley. Care is needed at the railway crossing before finishing back at the Moors Centre.

DANBY, ESKDALE & THE PANNIERMAN'S CAUSEWAY

DISTANCE: 11.5KM/7.1MILES **» TOTAL ASCENT:** 300M/984FT **» START GR:** NZ 717083 **» TIME:** ALLOW 3 HOURS **MAP:** OS EXPLORER OL26 NORTH YORK MOORS WESTERN AREA **» REFRESHMENTS:** DANBY MOORS CENTRE, STONEHOUSE BAKERY, DUKE OF WELLINGTON – ALL DANBY; ESKDALE INN, ESKDALE ARMS, CASTLETON TEA ROOMS – ALL CASTLETON; THE FOX & HOUNDS, AINTHORPE **» NAVIGATION:** STRAIGHTFORWARD. PATHS AND BRIDLEWAYS ARE MARKED BUT TAKE CARE ON THE PANNIERMAN'S CAUSEWAY.

CASTLETON

11 DANBY, ESKDALE & THE PANNIERMAN'S CAUSEWAY

Directions – Danby, Eskdale & The Pannierman's Causeway

❺ Leave the car park **turning right** for 50m to the bottom of the bank at the road junction. Cross opposite to a gate at the far side signed *Public Footpath*. This leads up the hill for 330m to another gate.

2 Go **straight ahead** at the gate onto a grassy track with a wall to your left. Stay with this track as it bends to the right after 120m down the hill to gate into woods. Keep **straight ahead** after the gate ignoring another track to the left. Follow the track through the woods eventually coming to a footbridge.

3 Cross the bridge and **turn left** to a stile over a wall. The track now climbs up through bracken for 500m to a wall corner. **Keep left** at the corner following a track which joins a wider track, ignoring a gate to a farm. This track **bears left** over Clither Beck passing the farm just to the north.

4 At a wall corner 280m after the beck crossing **turn left** with a wall on a narrow path leading to a road. **Turn left** on the road for 120m. **Turn right** here onto a narrow path. Stay with this path for 600m to a bridleway crossing. Go **straight ahead** for another 100m crossing a stream and then **immediately turn left** downhill towards buildings.

5 The route is now marked with wooden posts painted white and blue on top. These posts lead the way down past Rosedale Intake through a gate to a ford through the stream at the bottom. 150m after crossing the stream **turn left** at a single gate with a blue waymarker and walk across a field, **turning left again** at gate.

6 About 140m after the gate at the top of the hill keep **straight ahead** over a track picking up a bridleway between walls. Stay with this track for 260m down to a wall corner and take the **right fork**. After 400m at a gate **keep right** on a track angling down towards Danby Park woods. **Turn right** on a track to a gate into woods and follow a good track through the woods to Park Nook.

7 At Park Nook there are the remains of an old tramway bridge. **Turn left** here to the road. **Turn left** at a road passing the railway station and Eskdale Arms, up the hill and into Castleton. At the junction in Castleton **turn left**, passing a lane after 150m. Then, after another 150m and a line of cottages, **turn right** onto a public footpath.

8 Drop to a bridge and **keep left** on a grassy track past the memorial. 60m after the memorial **turn right** onto a lane for 40m to Howe Farm. **Turn left** into the farm, crossing a gravel yard to a gate, and follow markers across a field and stile to Longlands Lane. **Turn left** for 50m then **right** through an iron gate marked with *Public Footpath* sign.

9 Cross farmyard to a stile and follow the footpath along a ditch. Follow the markers, always with the ditch to your left, to a lane. **Turn right** at the lane and make a **quick right** at the wall corner up a wide grass track for 140m, **turning left** at the top to The Fox & Hounds pub. **Turn left** down the road for 100m then **turn right** through a double gate onto a wide track signposted *Public Footpath*.

10 Follow this track for 200m to a point at two gates: take the **left** over a stile and **turn right** after 50m. Follow the waymarkers and **turn left** alongside the sports field to road. **Turn right** and then after 220m **turn left** through a single gate signposted *Danby via Moors Centre*. Follow this path, taking care crossing the railway, back to the car park.

THE MOORS CENTRE

NORTH YORK MOORS RAILWAY IN NEWTON DALE PHOTO: TONY HARKER

12 Levisham & the Hole of Horcum

13.5km/8.4miles

Fantastic scenery in the Hole of Horcum and wonderful views over Newton Dale.

Levisham Station » Yorfalls Wood » Skelton Tower » Levisham Moor » Hole of Horcum » Levisham Brow » Levisham » Levisham Station

Start

Levisham Railway Station. Parking (with a donation box) at the station. GR: SE 817910.

The Walk

The walk through the Hole of Horcum is a moors classic, but by extending the walk to Levisham and into Cropton Forest we touch on some less frequented footpaths. What's more, the views from Skelton Tower into Newton Dale and the view into the Hole of Horcum must be two of the top five views on the moors.

Starting from the station we take a short walk through the forest before climbing up through the bracken onto the moor above Yorfalls Wood. Here the views into Newton Dale are terrific and get better as you approach Skelton Tower. Easy moorland walking and a short climb takes us to the top edge of the expanse of the sunken Hole of Horcum. The path drops down into this beautiful valley heading south passing Dundale Griff and then onto the wooded walk into Levisham Village. From the village we cross a couple of fields, skirt the woods and are again rewarded with more great views of Newton Dale before dropping into the valley and a return to the station.

LEVISHAM & THE HOLE OF HORCUM

DISTANCE: 13.5KM/8.4MILES » **TOTAL ASCENT:** 500M/1,640FT » **START GR:** SE 817910 » **TIME:** ALLOW 4 HOURS **MAP:** OS EXPLORER OL27 NORTH YORK MOORS EASTERN AREA » **REFRESHMENTS:** THE MOORS TEA ROOM, LEVISHAM STATION; THE HORSEHOE INN, LEVISHAM » **NAVIGATION:** MOSTLY EASY AND WELL MARKED. CARE IS NEEDED ON CLIMB OVER HAWNBY MOOR.

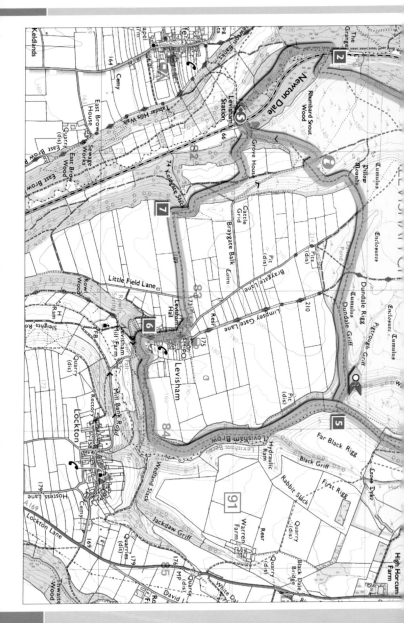

12 LEVISHAM & THE HOLE OF HORCUM

Directions – Levisham & the Hole of Horcum

❻ From the station car park **turn left** onto the lane over the railway crossing. After 900m **turn right** down steps to a wooden bridge signposted *Newtondale Halt via Moors*.

2 Go through the gate and follow the path (signposted *Levisham Station Walk*) up through the bracken bending sharp left after 120m. This leads up to the moor edge. At the edge stay with the Levisham Station Walk on a path following the escarpment edge over Yorfalls Wood. As the wall falls away to the left, the track forks: **fork right** towards Skelton Tower.

3 **Turn right** at the tower still keeping to the edge and follow the path round Levisham Bottoms, **ignoring** the Levisham Station Walk sign bearing off to the left, all the way round to the A169 (**ignore** any other paths turning off) – a drop to the left and hillside to the right most of the way. A short steep climb leads to the corner of the road to the top of the Hole Of Horcum.

4 **Turn left** at the top gate and then **quick right** over a stile and take the well-trodden grassy footpath down the drop into the 'Hole'. Just after the Low Horcum buildings **keep right** at the fork and continue down the valley for 700m and again take the **right fork**. Cross bridge after 800m and cross the stream to a signpost.

> **OR** For a shorter route through Dundale Griff **turn right** here for 1km to a track and signpost. Keep **straight ahead** for 460m to a wall corner. Track the wall for 200m and then keep **straight ahead** for another 60m to a hillside edge. **Turn left** dropping down the edge to the road. **Turn right** to the station.

5 To continue on the main route go **straight ahead** signposted *Levisham*. The path climbs through bracken at first and then contours around the woods and the valley leading to a road. **Turn right** to Levisham Village.

6 Just before The Horsehoe Inn, and road bend, a lane turns off left. **Follow this** for 300m to where the lane bears sharp left. **Turn off the road** onto a footpath crossing two fields with a wall to right. At the bottom of the second field the path bears right to a stile leading into woods.

7 This path will lead you round the top of Keldgate before dropping to a field corner. **Turn off left** over a stile and then **turn immediate right** along the fence. Follow the field round left (yellow arrows) down to the bottom of the field. Go **straight ahead** through a single gate into woods. A short walk through the woods leads to a road. **Turn left** to return back to the station.

HOLE OF HORCUM PHOTO: TONY HARKER

FELLED FOREST EAST SIDE OF GLAISDALE PHOTO: TONY HARKER

13 Beggers Bridge & Egton High Moor   14km/8.7miles

High moor, wonderful woodland and easy going.

Beggers Bridge » East Arncliff Wood » Delves » Grange Head Farm » Egton High Moor » Wain Hill » Smith's Lane » Beggers Bridge

Start

Beggers Bridge. Parking next to Beggers Bridge and under the arches. GR: NZ 784054.

The Walk

This is a fantastic circular walk with high moors and deep dales, starting from the famous Beggers Bridge (built 1619) which straddles the River Esk close to Glaisdale railway station. Although a lofty height of 300m is gained on Egton High Moor, the climbing during the walk is relatively easy without any difficult, sharp uphills. The path on the east side of Glaisdale offers fantastic views into the Glaisdale valley, especially when the bracken is fully grown and the heather is in full bloom.

Leaving the bridge we begin the walk through the delightful East Arnecliff Wood on an ancient paved packhorse route. After lovely meadow walking over Butler Beck the track takes us towards Grange Head Farm, nestled high up the valley.

We turn onto the moor at this point, using our map/GPS to carefully keep to the path which leads to the firm track over Egton High Moor. Views north down the valley into Eskdale are glorious and the track over the moor is just short enough to not become too tiresome. A short detour could be made to the trig point on Pike Hill and the pond a little further on.

After a short road section we turn over moor again heading for the Glaisdale valley. The track follows a shallow gully for most of the descent and we have to pick our way carefully in and out of the gully to make any headway. We eventually find the path which takes us along the east side of Glaisdale valley: it is narrow but easy to follow alongside the low wall over which there are wonderful views across the valley to Glaisdale Rigg. We finish on a broad track descent back through East Arnecliff Wood.

BEGGERS BRIDGE & EGTON HIGH MOOR

DISTANCE: 14KM/8.7MILES » TOTAL ASCENT: 440M/1,443FT » START GR: NZ 784054 » TIME: ALLOW 4 HOURS MAP: OS EXPLORER OL27 NORTH YORK MOORS EASTERN AREA » REFRESHMENTS: THE ARNCLIFFE ARMS, GLAISDALE; POST OFFICE & SHOP, GLAISDALE » NAVIGATION: CARE NEEDED ON THE CLIMB ABOVE GRANGE HEAD FARM AND ON THE MOOR BELOW BROWN HILL.

13 BEGGERS BRIDGE & EGTON HIGH MOOR

Directions – Beggers Bridge & Egton High Moor

↦ Cross the narrow Glaisdale Beck via the footbridge leading to a short stepped climb into East Arncliff Wood. Stay with this easy to follow path (the *Esk Valley Walk*) all the way through the wood to the lane.

2 **Turn right** at the lane following the road uphill. At the hilltop **turn left** through a gate onto a narrow path descending through woods. Keep **straight ahead** at single and double gates, keeping the tree line to your left. Cross the stream via a footbridge and then **aim slightly left** uphill to a wall corner under a telegraph pole. Follow a track between trees to a bridleway. **Turn right** onto the track leading to Hall Grange Farm.

3 Go **straight ahead** through the farm on a firm track. Stay with this track for 1.7km along the edge of the woods to a track bend at Grange Head Farm. As the track bends right to the farm **turn left** through a gate onto the moor. Follow this double track which stays visible, but only just. 20m after the gate **fork left** to signpost. Stay with this track passing another signpost and climb up to a stile at a fence.

4 Shortly after the fence the track bends right and drops into a shallow gully. Follow the line of the gully southwest. The track becomes vague for 200m. Keep heading southwest aiming for a wide green section of track 300m ahead, just in front of a line of wooden shooting hides. (If visibility is poor you may need to take a compass bearing or use GPS for navigation.) As you approach the hides the track joins a double shooting track running parallel with the bridleway. Stay on the track and follow this onto Egton High Moor, passing Pike Hill and onto the Egton road.

5 **Turn right** on the road for 560m and then **turn left** onto bridleway. Keep **straight ahead** at the wall corner following the blue bridleway marker. After passing a large cairn to the left the track drops into a shallow gully. Follow the line of the gully down the hillside. As the gully turns left towards the trees look out for a narrow path **turning off right** towards the wall.

6 Now stay with this path for 1.5km, easy to follow and always tracking the wall. The path leads to a wider track and a short climb through a gap in the forest to the Egton road. **Turn left** onto the road for 700m and then **turn left** into a narrow lane. Follow the lane which turns to track past Snowdon Nab Farm and leads back down to Beggers Bridge.

THE PATH ALONG IBURNDALE BECK

14 Sleights & the Esk Valley

15km/9.3miles

An ancient walkway to the trains at Grosmont and fantastic views towards Whitby.

Sleights » Back Wood » Grosmont » Fair Head Lane » Lowther's Crag » Blue Bank » Iburndale Beck » Iburndale » Sleights

---

Start

Sleights Railway Station. Small car park near station, or roadside parking at the station. GR NZ 867080.

The Walk

Apart from the road climb out of Grosmont this is a relatively easy walk. The first half is dominated by views into the Esk Valley along the partly paved bridleway to Grosmont, and the return leg by the vast panorama over to Whitby and the North Sea. The last section alongside Iburndale Beck is a delight.

We begin on the Esk Valley Way, passing Grove Hall, following the route of an old paved causeway – clearly evident for much of the four miles towards Grosmont. Ever changing terrain of meadows and deep woods holds our interest with the glimpse of a steam train always a possibility. After Grosmont we leave the hustle and steam

below as we complete 90% of the day's ascent up Fair Head Lane. After a breather the quarry track across the moor above Lowther's Crag rewards hard work with vast views towards Whitby and the coastline. Although never higher than 260m the panorama to the northeast gives the impression that we are at a far greater elevation. The walk is completed along the lovely path following the line of Iburndale Beck crossing stepping stones and edging along the stream's meanders.

SLEIGHTS & THE ESK VALLEY

DISTANCE: 15KM/9.3MILES » **TOTAL ASCENT:** 450M/1,476FT » **START GR:** NZ 867080 » **TIME:** ALLOW 4 HOURS **MAP:** OS EXPLORER OL27 NORTH YORK MOORS EASTERN AREA » **REFRESHMENTS:** THREE TEA ROOMS IN GROSMONT; THE PLOUGH, THE SALMON LEAP – SLEIGHTS; STATION TAVERN, GROSMONT » **NAVIGATION:** MOSTLY EASY AND WELL MARKED.

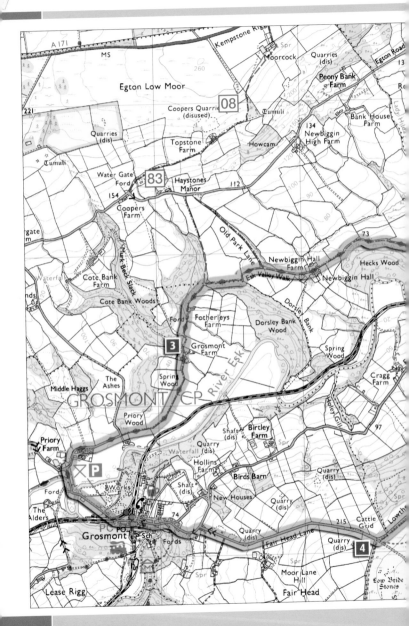

14 SLEIGHTS & THE ESK VALLEY

Directions – Sleights & the Esk Valley

⑥➤ The walk can be started either in Sleights or Grosmont: I've opted to start in Sleights, with parking at the railway station. Go through the station gate, crossing the lines to the footpath over the bridge. **Turn left** at the lane to the A169. Walk **straight ahead** to the lane signposted *Public Bridleway*.

2 Follow this lane for 700m to a point after the sharp bend over bridge. 50m uphill **turn left** at *Public Bridleway* sign through a single gate onto a paved path into a field. This is part of the Esk Valley Way and is well marked throughout. Follow it towards Grosmont. **Note**: the only points where a wrong turning could be made are:

    a) At Thistle Grove: **turn left** onto the track signposted *Grosmont*.
    b) In Back Wood: when you hit the farm track **turn right** and **quick left**
        signposted *Public Bridleway*.
    c) After Newbiggin Farm: as the track bends right, keep **straight ahead**
        onto path between fences signposted *Public Bridleway*.
    d) In Dorsley Wood: after single gate, **keep left** at path T-junction
        signposted *Public Bridleway*.

3 From Grosmont Farm follow the farm road through to the Egton road. **Turn left** here for 700m to Grosmont. Keep **straight ahead** over the railway crossing and up the steep bank. Stay on this road for 1.7km, **keeping right** at the two road junctions.

4 Near the top of the climb cross the cattle grid and after another 120m **turn left** onto bridleway and wide firm track. After 350m **keep left** before quarry gate keeping to wall. Stay with this track to a point where it ends abruptly after 1km as the wall bends left. Keep **straight ahead** on track over heather as it turns to single track. At fork after 300m aim for standing stone on ridge. As the path nears the old quarry **keep right** at fork around the quarry edge and then **straight ahead** to a quarry basin after 200m. Follow the rim of the quarry basin to the left, crossing a track, and keep straight ahead to a stile leading to the A169.

5 Cross the road **turning right** in the car park. Take the path at the Public Footpath sign. **Ignore** double gate ahead and **almost immediately fork left** towards the pylon. Cross stile and follow path downhill to road. At the road **turn right** down steep twisting road for 700m.

6 **Turn left** at junction signposted *Alum House*. Follow this lane all the way for another 700m through to the concrete ford near Throstle Nest. Cross ford and **turn right** to stepping stones. Follow footpath marked *No entry to cars and motorbikes*. Stay with this path tracking the stream and more stepping stones well marked all the way through to Iburndale.

7 In Iburndale **turn left** over the bridge and then **immediate right** between garden fences picking up path marked *Public Footpath*. At T-junction **turn right** and then **left** before bridge onto lane signposted *Public Bridleway*. Follow lane back to the station.

LOW DALE

MOORLAND TRACK NEAR MARY MAGDALENE WELL

15 **Hutton-le-Hole** & **Lastingham**   16km/10miles

This is a classic moorland walk through heather and bracken with fine views throughout.

Hutton-le-Hole » Hutton Ridge » High Snapes » Ana Cross » Askew Rigg » Lastingham » Hutton-le-Hole

Start

Hutton-le-Hole car park. GR: SE 704901.

The Walk

This is predominantly a moorland walk circling Spaunton Moor. The walk along the eastern flanks through the waist high bracken is wonderful with views over to Cropton Forest. The path over Askew Ridge and crossing Tranmire Beck is pleasant and gives a feeling of total isolation, yet it is within one mile of a road.

The long gradual climb up Hutton Ridge gets us started on this walk. This is by no means a tedious climb. The path is mostly grass and if you keep looking over your left shoulder there are some nice views over the bottom end of Farndale. However, we do pick up a track on High Snapes which takes us over the fords of Loskey Ridge.

Here we leave the track and cross Loskey Beck a little upstream to pick up the footpath over the moor to the road. A short walk on the road brings us to the top of Chimney Bank. Here, we take the wide track south passing Ana Cross and then turn east dropping down towards Hollins Farm. A good path leads south through the bracken before we take the footpath cutting southwest over Askew Rigg and Tranmire Beck. We finish with a short road section and then a well marked footpath.

HUTTON–LE–HOLE & LASTINGHAM

DISTANCE: 16KM/10MILES » **TOTAL ASCENT:** 370M/1,213FT » **START GR:** SE 704901 » **TIME:** ALLOW 4 HOURS **MAP:** OS EXPLORER OL26 NORTH YORK MOORS WESTERN AREA & OL27 NORTH YORK MOORS EASTERN AREA » **REFRESHMENTS:** THE FORGE TEA ROOMS, THE LION INN, HUTTON-LE-HOLE; THE BLACKSMITHS ARMS, LASTINGHAM » **NAVIGATION:** STRAIGHTFORWARD.

ANA CROSS

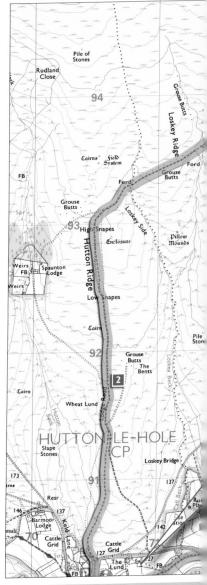

15 HUTTON-LE-HOLE & LASTINGHAM

Directions — Hutton-le-Hole & Lastingham

↱ **Turn right** out of the car park and then **left** after 230m onto a footpath. After a gate take the grassy track on the **right**. Follow this for 1km to a tarmac track and **turn left**.

2 After 400m **turn right** at a waymarker onto a footpath. After 1.3km **turn right** onto a track. At the second valley, after 930m, **turn left**. Follow the stream for 20m and then cross to the footpath opposite. Aim for a wide grassy area (20m wide) above a shooting butt. Follow this path to the road.

3 **Turn left** on the road for 560m and then **right** onto a track passing Ana Cross to the right. 470m after the Cross **turn left** at cross tracks. Track goes narrow after pit (300m) bending to left and dropping to old quarry after 550m. **Turn right** through a gap and then **left** at a grass track dropping to a wall corner.

4 **Turn right** on a wide track for 2.7km. **Turn right** onto a footpath with waymarker. After 900m keep **straight ahead** over a track onto a footpath. Cross the stream (Tranmire Beck) after 450m. Follow the track up a steep climb onto wide pasture. Keep with line of fence to a track junction with signpost and bench.

5 Go **straight ahead** past a bench down to a stream. Follow the path alongside the wall passing Camomile Farm to the road. **Turn right** at the road and after 780m **turn left** at *Public Footpath* sign. Follow footpath through a range of gates to Hutton-le-Hole village. **Turn right** and follow road back to car park.

PAVED CAUSEWAY ON LEALHOLM RIGG *PHOTO: TONY HARKER*

16 Ugthorpe & Lealholm

16km/10miles

Explore the quiet north east corner of the moors and the quaint Lealholm village deep in the Esk Valley.

Ugthorpe » Coquet Nook » Stonegate Beck » Lealholm » Lealholm Rigg » Traveller's Rest Farm » Ugthorpe

Start

Ugthorpe village. Plenty of roadside parking. GR: NZ 794112.

The Walk

Starting at Ugthorpe, an off the beaten track linear village, you can sense that this could be one of those never-see-another-soul walks. The route takes us south into the Esk Valley over farmland and pastures, while the return leg to Ugthorpe is predominantly moorland and can be quite wild and remote reflecting the moody atmosphere of the moors in this area.

We start by making use of farm tracks and footpaths past Coquet Nook to the busy A171. Easy lane walking with fine views of the Esk Valley leads past Thornhill Farm and the lovely crossing of Stonegate Beck.

A steep climb to Hall Park Farm brings on the descent into the Esk Valley where we meet an easy-going track which runs with the railway into the picturesque village of Lealholm. There are plenty of options for refreshments here before we begin the return leg along the north edge of the railway up Elm Ridge.

Classic moorland footpaths take us high onto Lealholm Rigg and its paved causeway. A little more road walking leads us across a shallow valley to meet the track over the moor to the A171. We finish on a long farm track from Traveller's Rest Farm back into Ugthorpe.

UGTHORPE & LEALHOLM

DISTANCE: 16KM/10MILES » TOTAL ASCENT: 390M/1,279FT » START GR: NZ 794112 » TIME: ALLOW 4 HOURS MAP: OS EXPLORER OL27 NORTH YORK MOORS EASTERN AREA » REFRESHMENTS: BLACK BULL INN, POST OFFICE & CONVENIENCE STORE, UGTHORPE; THE BECK VIEW, SHEPHERDS HALL – BOTH LEALHOLM » NAVIGATION: MOSTLY EASY AND WELL MARKED.

PHOTO: TONY HARKER

16 UGTHORPE & LEALHOLM

Directions – Ugthorpe & Lealholm

⑤▸ Walk to the eastern end of the village and **turn right** at the church onto a tarmac lane and follow this through to the road at Ugthorpe Grange. Keep **straight ahead** at the road and follow it to Biggin House. **Turn right** into the field, keeping the fence to the left. Walk **straight ahead** at the gate and, 50m after the fence corner at the point where a path crosses, **turn left** onto the path to a stile. Follow path to Coquet Nook and farm lane to A171.

2 **Turn right** and, after 150m, **turn left**. **Turn left** once again at the crossroads. After 200m **turn right** at *Public Footpath* sign into field, keeping fence to your left. At far side of field go through gate and **turn immediate left** and follow fence around side of farm to stile leading to farm lane.

3 Follow lane **right** and **turn left** to Howe House. Go through gate and **turn right** down field keeping fence and ditch to right. Pass the fence and stile and take the path **right** to Westonby Farm. Follow farm lane to road.

4 **Turn left** for 200m and then **turn right** down lane bridleway. This leads to Thornhill Farm. **Turn left** at farm (signposted) passing shed to right. At end of farm **turn left** through gate dropping into field. **Don't** aim for the double gate in view but cross the field to the wooded beck in the western corner and the single gate leading to the path through the trees. Follow this path down to the bridge and ford.

5 Go through the gate and follow the path uphill, with fence/trees to the right, to Hall Park Farm. At the farm **turn left** onto the farm lane and follow it around corner. When the lane turns sharp right **go left** dropping down across verge to gate. Follow path around the edge of Hill House Farm **ignoring** the bridleway sign pointing down the sharp valley. At far side of farm the path drops down through a gate leading to the road.

6 At the road **turn left** and then **immediately right** onto a bridleway across an open field. Aim over the knoll towards trees. Drop downhill, keeping woods to the right, ignoring gate. Follow track under railway to farmyard. **Turn right** in farmyard onto farm lane leading into Lealholm. At Lealholm **turn right** and follow the road up the bank over the railway.

7   **Turn left** after the bridge to the station. After the station **fork right** and follow the track alongside the shallow valley. **Bend right** following the track (keeping away from wall), bending right at the bottom over stream. Follow this track uphill with a line of trees to the right. At the end of trees **turn left** and follow this track for 350m to a farm track. **Turn right** and follow this to the road. **Turn right**.

8   At the road corner after 200m go **straight ahead** onto a paved causeway bridleway. Stay with this path over Lealholm Rigg for 800m. At a point where the paving stops **turn left** onto an indistinct path over heather. Cross track and keep **straight ahead** at *Public Bridleway* sign keeping the shallow gully to the right. Cross the moor picking up a double track leading to the road.

9   **Turn right** for 300m and then **left** at road junction. Follow the road across the valley to Woodhill House at the top of the bank. Keep following road past left-hand bend and after 150m **turn right** at a gate. Follow through second gate towards a stream. **Bear left** at the stream and follow a narrow path over a flagstone bridge. After 200m go through a gate to the **right** onto a path tracking the fence uphill to a point where the wall/fence bends to the right.

10   From the wall/fence corner keep **straight ahead**. This is a short section of indistinct grassland. Aim for the lane to Travellers Rest Farm some 500m ahead. Cross the stile and field to the A171. **Go straight over** onto the lane to the farm. Stay on the track through a gate after the farm and follow this all the way back to Ugthorpe.

PATH ALONG DISMANTLED RAILWAY ON BLAKEY RIDGE PHOTO: TONY HARKER

17 Blakey Ridge & Farndale

18km/11.2miles

This is moorland walking at its best. Narrow trails through the heather broken only by the crossing of the deep, green Farndale valley.

The Lion Inn » Flat Howe » Farndale Moor » Gill Beck » Rudland Rigg » Monket House Crags » Low Blakey Moor » The Lion Inn

Start

The Lion Inn on Blakey Ridge (please only park here with permission). Alternative parking in rough car park 600m south of Inn. GR: SE 679996.

The Walk

Blakey Ridge sits in the middle of the National Park dissecting Farndale and Rosedale. The old iron ore railway acts as an umbilical cord tying the two valleys together where it once crossed via a bridge between the two valleys just south of The Lion Inn. The Inn nestles just below Cockpit Howe, a Neolithic burial mound, and it can be dated back to 1553. An interesting history of the Inn can be found on its website (www.lionblakey.co.uk).

The head of Farndale is less well known than the touristy bits on the famous Daffodil Walk, except of course for the old railway that wriggles along its northern contours. We touch on both the Daffodil Walk and railway on this route but only briefly as our route explores some of the less well known paths with a surprise waterfall thrown in as a bonus.

The views into Farndale are fantastic, particularly from the east side. You will need to navigate some parts of this walk carefully and will want to linger above the deep ravine of Gill Beck and its un-named waterfall. This is truly a moorland walk packed with nice surprises.

BLAKEY RIDGE & FARNDALE

DISTANCE: 18KM/11.2MILES » **TOTAL ASCENT:** 560M/1,837FT » **START GR:** SE 679996 » **TIME:** ALLOW 5 HOURS **MAP:** OS EXPLORER OL26 NORTH YORK MOORS WESTERN AREA » **REFRESHMENTS:** THE LION INN, BLAKEY RIDGE; FEVERSHAM ARMS, CHURCH HOUSES; THE DAFFY CAFFY, FARNDALE; CASTLETON TEA ROOMS, CASTLETON » **NAVIGATION:** REGULAR MAP CHECKING REQUIRED.

CONTINUES ON PAGE 110

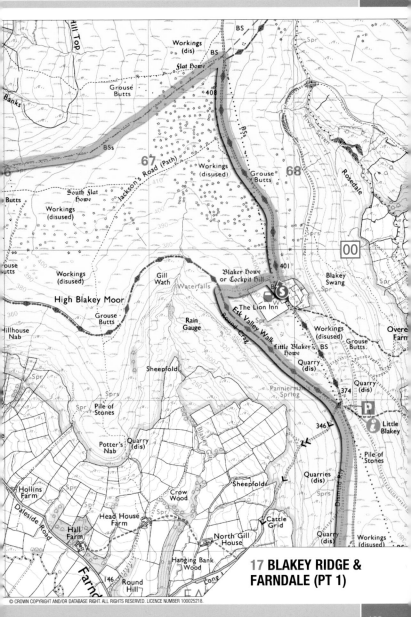

17 BLAKEY RIDGE & FARNDALE (PT 1)

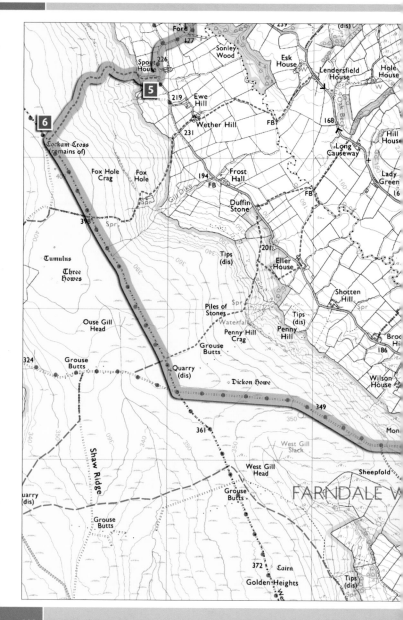

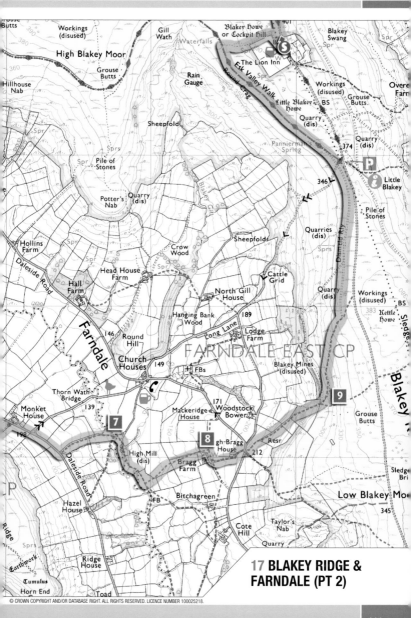

17 BLAKEY RIDGE & FARNDALE (PT 2)

Directions — Blakey Ridge & Farndale

➒ Leave The Lion Inn car park and **turn left** on the road towards Castleton. After 1.6km **turn left** at a track marked with a large standing stone (opposite a bridleway). **Turn left** after 20m onto a wide track which narrows. Follow this track/path for 2km through to the old railway.

2 **Turn right** on the railway for 1.3km to a point where the railway just bends left. About 100m before a wooden fence at the side of the railway **turn left** at a stream bordered with reeds. **Note**: the path is erroneously marked on maps running down the east side of the stream but as it does not exist it is easier to follow the west bank of the stream.

3 Pick up the path just before the line of trees and cross the stream. After 100m cross another stream and join double track following the edge of the ravine. Follow the track through a wall and down to a stile to a farm lane. **Turn left** for 150m and then before the bridge **turn right** through a gate onto a wide grassy lane.

4 Follow the lane down between a wall and stream **bearing right** at the bottom over a footbridge. Stay on a track between walls uphill to a farm lane. **Turn left** and then, after just 220m, as the lane bears right and drops at a wall corner, **turn right** onto a track marked with a *Public Footpath* sign.

5 The track leads to gate in a corner after 170m. Go through the gate and **bear right** through the bracken. At this point the path follows the route of a shallow gully which meanders up the hillside. It is easier to follow a path just to the right of the gully as the gully makes many turns eventually leading to a path below two TV aerials on the 360m contour. Keep to the south of the aerials where there is still a navigable path climbing towards Rutland Rigg.

6 **Turn left** onto a wide track – Rudland Rigg – and follow the Rigg south for 1.9km **turning left** at the main track crossroads. This track leads down to the valley road and Monket House. **Turn right** at the road passing a lane to left. After 400m **turn left** at a footpath signed *Church Houses* over a stile keeping the wall to the left. Follow this path down the hill and over a stile. Towards the bottom the path angles right away from a stream towards the River Dove and footbridge.

7 Cross the bridge and **turn right** to follow a path across a field to a farm lane. Pass through the buildings of High Mill and walk **straight ahead** onto a paved path. 200m after a gate **turn left** across a field aiming for a gap between a wall and fence. **Turn left** at a gate under a tree onto a good path leading to a track and Bragg Farm. As the track bends right to the farm **keep left** through a gate **turning right** at the next gate around the top of the farm.

8 Go through the farmyard and then **left** up farm track towards road. Cross road through gate onto path across fields. Stay with wall for 360m to a double gate and **angle slightly right** uphill towards shallow gully leading to moor gate. Go **straight ahead** for 70m and **turn left** through reeds (level with tree on right) picking up a good narrow path.

9 Follow this path leading up the hillside, bending to the right after 350m near the crest. 10m over the crest **turn left** onto a path – the disused railway – along the embankment. Follow this the old railway for almost 1km to the road. Cross the road continuing on the old railway for another 1km and **turn right** at the National Park information board. Follow this path up alongside the wall to Cockpit Hill and **turn right** to return to The Lion Inn.

LOW BLAKEY MOOR PHOTO: TONY HARKER

18 **Goathland & Grosmont** 18km/11.2miles

If ever there was a walk with a bit of everything this is it! Not so much high moorland but a variety of paths, tracks, pasture, woodland and lively moorland villages.

Mallyan Spout Hotel » Abbot's House » Whinstone Ridge » Spa Hill Slack » Grosmont » River Esk » Castle Hill » Beck Hole » Mallyan Spout » Mallyan Spout Hotel

Start

Mallyan Spout Hotel. GR: NZ 827007.

The Walk

Deep valleys, woodland, moorland, meadows, steam engines, and one of the National Park's famous waterfalls. This 18km walk is the longer of the two from Goathland and explores the Moors to the north and east of the village. The terrain and views change frequently and you'll never be far from the sound of steam engines, even deep down in Spa Hill Slack.

We leave Mallyan Spout Hotel, just south of Goathland, following a well-marked footpath to the campsite just west of Abbot's House. From here we cross to the east of the railway and head north towards Goathland. Views open out over to Two Howes Rigg and there is a great stretch of open railway so watch out for steam locomotives. A nice easy going track takes us through the heather towards Whinstone Ridge, after which hard track leads to the lovely drop into Spa Hill Slack.

We leave this path after a short climb following the footpath past Moor Lane Farm and then onto the road which takes us down into Grosmont.

Any steam train enthusiast will want to linger here and watch the locomotives shunting back and forth. We leave Grosmont on a wide valley track passing the old tollhouse before crossing the River Esk over one of its widest footbridges and then following a network of footpaths up towards Castle Hill. Lovely views open up across the valley to the east – our outward route – and further south into Goathland. A pleasant path takes us easily down the hill again through the forest to the old railway walk and Beck Hole. We finish along the wonderful path running alongside West Beck towards Mallyan Spout with a final climb up to the Hotel – including sixty-nine steps!

GOATHLAND & GROSMONT

DISTANCE: 18KM/11.2MILES » **TOTAL ASCENT:** 530M/1,738FT » **START GR:** NZ 827007 » **TIME:** ALLOW 4.5 HOURS **MAP:** OS EXPLORER OL27 NORTH YORK MOORS EASTERN AREA » **REFRESHMENTS:** THE MOORS TEA ROOM, GOATHLAND TEA ROOMS, THE GOATHLAND ARMS, THE INN ON THE MOORS, THE MALLYAN SPOUT HOTEL, POST OFFICE & GIFT SHOPS, PLENTY OF GOOD QUALITY B&BS – ALL GOATHLAND; BIRCH HALL INN – BECK HOLE » **NAVIGATION:** MOSTLY EASY AND WELL MARKED.

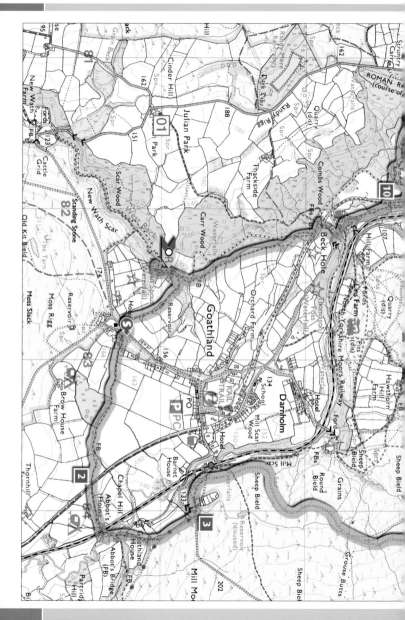

18 GOATHLAND & GROSMONT

Directions – Goathland & Grosmont

❺ From the Mallyan Spout Hotel cross the road to a track and a *Public Footpath* sign leading to a gate. Go through the gate onto a footpath across fields through a succession of gates and stiles. After the last stile a **right turn** leads into a small caravan park.

2 Join the track through the park **bearing left**, crossing the old railway path and alongside another camping field signposted *Abbot's House*. The track leads under a bridge. **Turn left** immediately before the building crossing a small field to a footbridge. After the bridge a double gate leads to a path climbing alongside a wall. Follow this straight up the hill until you reach the tarmac lane. Follow the lane to the Goathland road.

3 **Turn left** for 30m and then **right** on a gravel track and **quick left** onto a grassy footpath marked with *Public Footpath* sign. Follow this path for 150m and **turn right** onto double track. Stay with this track for 2.1km across the moor to the Beck Hole road.

4 **Turn left** at the road and after 400m **turn right** onto signed *Public Bridleway* to Greenlands Farm. Follow the track to the farm and pass the farm **to the right** through two double gates marked with yellow arrows. A good path leads down to Lythe Beck in Spa Hill Slack.

5 Cross the stream and climb the hill, **the path now a little indistinct**. Keep the wall on the left and, shortly after passing a small stone building, **turn left** through a double gate marked with a Public Footpath arrow. Follow path to a farm lane and the road. **Turn left** on the road into Grosmont, **keeping left** at two junctions.

6 Keep **straight ahead** at level crossing and then 500m after the village, after the road bends right, **turn left** onto a wide track signposted *Egton Bridge 1½ miles*. After the track bends under the railway pass the old tollhouse and then **turn left** at white farm onto footpath. Pass the farm through gates to the right to the bottom of the field. **Turn right** over a long footbridge.

7 Follow a shallow stream to a bridleway, **turning right** to a gate. Go through the gate and climb a steep hill to Honey Bee Nest Cottage. Pass by the cottage and join a tarmac lane continuing up the hill to the road.

8 Go straight over the road and join a footpath gently climbing over fields to Low Burrows and then a farm lane to the road. **Turn right** at the road. After 240m, where the road bends right at the top of a climb, **bear left** onto a bridleway. This leads through a succession of fields before coming to the Goathland road via a gate in a field corner.

9 **Turn left** at the road. **Turn left** again after 300m (second footpath on the left) leading into forest. Follow the path downhill keeping **straight ahead** at the fork after 270m. At the bottom of the hill the path comes to a building on the left. **Ignore** the path straight ahead alongside the building and **take the next path to the right**. Follow this down alongside the stream to the railway walk.

10 **Turn right** and after 200m **turn left** down steps, bearing to the right. Follow this path through to the road and Beck Hole. **Turn right** at the pub and then **left** onto the railway walk again. After 70m **turn right** though a gate signposted *Mallyan*. Stay with this path for 1km to the path junction below the Mallyan Spout Hotel.

OR To visit the waterfall, continue **straight ahead** for 130m.

To finish **turn left** up the hill and sixty-nine steps!

GROSMONT STATION PHOTO: TONY HARKER

SECTION 3

Coastal Walks

The North York Moors come to an abrupt end at the North Sea. Stretching 40km from Staithes to Scarborough this coastline is rugged with high cliffs, small fishing villages and spectacular scenery. This coastline has a legacy of mining and provides plenty of interest for geology enthusiasts. In places the moorland reaches to the cliff edge but generally there is a narrow belt of farmland between the moor and sea. Further to the west and the A169 there is a wide area of remote moorland broken further south by the expanse of the ever developing Dalby Forest complex.

THE VIEW TO RAVENSCAR FROM BOGGLE HOLE

19 Robin Hood's Bay

11.4km/7.1miles

Terrific coastal views with easy meadow walking.

Robin Hood's Bay » Raw » Brow Top » Oak Wood » Fyling Park » Robin Hood's Bay

Start

Road junction of Thorpe Lane and New Road/Whitby Road. GR: NZ 951053. Pay and display car parks at NZ 951052 and NZ 950054, or roadside parking near church NZ 948052.

The Walk

We leave the busy Robin Hood's Bay over a succession of fields picking up the Ramsdale Mill bridleway at Fyling Hall School. We reach the Mill via a good woodland track and then make a steady ascent through a narrow finger of woods. Eventually we reach the top of a long ridge with views over the whole of Robin Hood's Bay. With this fantastic panorama in front we wander over meadows reaching the quaint valley of Boggle Hole where we can even get refreshments in the Youth Hostel. We finish walking along the cliff tops with tea-rooms, pubs and shops waiting for us in the village.

ROBIN HOOD'S BAY

DISTANCE: 11.4KM/7.1MILES » **TOTAL ASCENT:** 400M/1,312FT » **START GR:** NZ 951053 » **TIME:** ALLOW 4 HOURS
MAP: OS EXPLORER OL27 NORTH YORK MOORS EASTERN AREA » **REFRESHMENTS:** COFFEE & TEA IS AVAILABLE AT BOGGLE HOLE YOUTH HOSTEL; LOTS OF OTHER PUBS, CAFÉS RESTAURANTS AND SHOPS IN ROBIN HOOD'S BAY » **NAVIGATION:** EASY AND WELL MARKED.

19 ROBIN HOOD'S BAY

Directions – Robin Hood's Bay

◐→ Set off on Thorpe Road signposted *Fylingthorpe*, passing the church on the right. 300m after the church, as the road bends left, **turn right** up steps and over the stile.

2 Follow the waymarkers over a series of stiles for 500m to a lane. **Turn left** on the lane and then **right** after 70m onto a rough track at Old Ridley. After 260m **turn left** through a gate leading to a private garden and follow the directions around the property perimeter to the road.

3 **Turn right** on the road for 160m and then **turn left** onto a track. After 400m **keep left** onto a path following the line of fence, rejoining track after 130m. Stay with the track for 100m to a junction and then keep **straight ahead** at a small post with a waymarker keeping to the line of the wall. Follow the track to the road. **Turn left** and **then right** at the road junction to Fyling Hall School. **Turn right** onto the track signposted *Public Bridleway*.

4 Follow this track for about 1.5km to Ramsdale Mill. From the mill stay with the track bending **left** and climbing to a building. Track bends to right and gate. Keep **straight ahead** through the gate onto a rocky track. Follow this for 800m through woods to a track junction.

5 **Turn left** to a gate and go **straight ahead** into a field: at the far end of the field **turn left** along the wall. After the gate follow the path over a field to a wooden signpost at gorse. **Turn right** onto a farm track leading for 1.3km to road. **Turn right** for 60m and then **left** at a footpath sign. Follow the path under railway and walk **straight ahead** at the next gate. At the second gate **turn left** on a path leading down to the bridge.

6 After the bridge follow the path bending up the field to the lane. **Turn right** at the lane, dropping to a ford. **Turn left** on a footpath leading to a bridge over a stream. Follow the lane up a steep climb, passing Mill Beck Farm, to a junction. **Turn left** to Boggle Hole.

7 At Boggle Hole **turn left** at signpost, crossing bridge and climbing steps on *Cleveland Way*. Follow *Cleveland Way* signs **keeping right** at track junction after 560m. At the village **turn left** on road up the lane to return to Robin Hood's Bay.

ROBIN HOOD'S BAY FROM THE MOOR ABOVE RAVENSCAR

20 Ravenscar: Moors & Coast 12.5km/7.8miles

A mix of moorland, meadow and coastal path with a deep steep-sided ravine crossing adding a little excitement to the walk.

Ravenscar » Howdale Moor » Cook House » How Dale » Stoupe Brow » Boggle Hole » Ravenscar

Start

Ravenscar (roadside parking only). GR: NZ 980015.

The Walk

Ravenscar is probably best known as the start (or end) of the 42-mile Lyke Wake Walk (www.lykewake.org), which crosses the Moors along its main east-west watershed. Perched over a hundred metres high on the cliff tops it was once the site of a grand new town plan that failed to materialise. Now it just boasts a sizable hotel, a coffee shop and a few houses. The views from Ravenscar north over the bay towards Robin Hood's Bay are fantastic and it's a view which remains with us for most of this walk.

We start by making our way along Robin Hood Lane picking up a footpath that winds its way up to the beacon. Now we are on Lyke Wake Walk territory and we follow a good track over Howdale Moor. As we approach the high point on this moor we see the wide and wild expanse of Fylingdales Moor and High Moor ahead. But we only have six more miles to go, not forty like the LWW walkers, and we turn off onto another track taking us towards Cook House.

Bearing northeast a firm gravel track edges along the moors boundary before dropping to Howdale Farm. After the farm we find ourselves on the edge of a deep ravine and drop steeply down to a bridge taking us safely to the far side before a climb around to Stoupe Browe. The scenery changes here as we round the hillside and the view opens up across to Robin Hood's Bay. We drop down under the railway bridge and cross Stoupe Beck with a sharp climb leading to the lane. From Boggle Hole we follow the Cleveland Way path and then turn off just after the alum works taking a more direct back to Ravenscar.

RAVENSCAR: MOORS & COAST

DISTANCE: 12.5KM/7.8MILES » **TOTAL ASCENT:** 390M/1,279FT » **START GR:** NZ 980015 » **TIME:** ALLOW 3.5 HOURS **MAP:** OS EXPLORER OL27 NORTH YORK MOORS EASTERN AREA » **REFRESHMENTS:** RAVENSCAR TEA ROOMS; COFFEE AND TEA IS AVAILABLE AT BOGGLE HOLE YOUTH HOSTEL » **NAVIGATION:** EASY AND WELL MARKED.

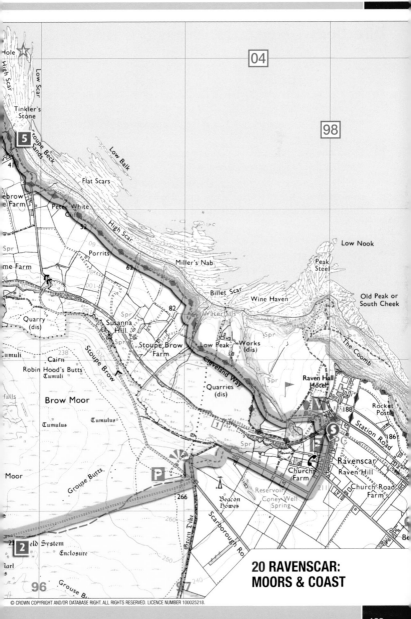

20 RAVENSCAR: MOORS & COAST

Directions – Ravenscar: Moors & Coast

➎ Begin on the road heading southwest towards the beacon. **Turn right** after 400m onto a lane and then **left** at a stile and waymarker. Follow the path uphill to another stile and **turn left** to a track junction. Follow the track signposted *Cleveland Way* for 1.3km.

2 **Turn right** at a waymarker on post and telegraph pole. After 1km **turn right** at a track junction (stones on left). Keep on this (white stone) track above the wall line **turning left** after another 900m to Howdale Farm. **Turn left** at the farm and continue **straight ahead** at a stile. Cross a field to a gate and **turn left** on a track for 100m. **Turn right** at a waymarker onto a narrow path down into the ravine.

3 Cross the footbridge and follow the waymaker **left** to a stile. **Bear right** after a stile leading to a garden and keep **straight ahead** to the lane. **Turn left** at junction leading under bridge. **Turn right** at a gate then **left** over fields with waymarkers for 600m to a bridge. **Bear right** after bridge for 5m then from fence corner walk **straight ahead** up hillside aiming for waymarker at top. Cross stile and **turn left** with waymarker keeping hedge to left leading to road.

4 **Turn right** passing car park and keep **straight ahead** down lane signposted *Boggle Hole Youth Hostel.* **Turn right** at *Cleveland Way* signpost up stepped climb. Path leads to lane. At bend **turn left** at gap in wall with *Cleveland Way* signpost.

5 Stay on the Cleveland Way for almost 2km to the alum works. 150m after alum works **keep left** at track junction, leaving the Cleveland Way. Cross stream after 400m and then **turn right** over stile onto footpath climbing to buildings. Follow path around top end of buildings leading to a drive. **Turn left** onto the lane and then **right** to the road and the finish.

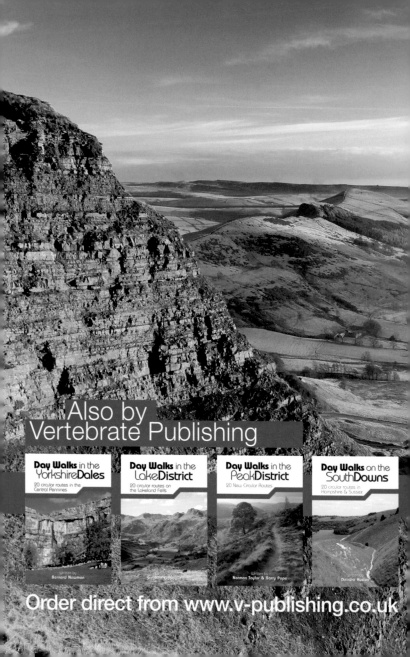

Also by
Vertebrate Publishing

Order direct from www.v-publishing.co.uk